IN SEARCH OF THOMAS SHEAHAN

T0167962

Maynooth Studies in Irish Local History

SERIES EDITOR   Raymond Gillespie

This is one of six new pamphlets in the Maynooth Studies in Irish Local History Series to be published in the year 2001 which brings the number published to forty. Like their predecessors most of the pamphlets are based on theses completed as part of the M.A. in local history programme in National University of Ireland, Maynooth. While the regions and time span which they cover are diverse, from Cork city to Tyrone, they all share a conviction that the exploration of the local past can shed light on the evolution of modern societies. They each demonstrate that understanding the evolution of local societies is important. The local worlds of Ireland in the past are as complex and sophisticated as the national framework in which they are set. The communities which peopled those local worlds, whether they be the inhabitants of large cities, housing on the edge of those cities or rural estates, shaped and were shaped by their environments to create a series of inter-locking worlds of considerable complexity. Those past worlds are best interpreted not through local administrative divisions, such as the county, but in human units: local places where communities of people lived and died. Untangling what held these communities together, and what drove them apart, gives us new insights into the world we have lost.

These pamphlets each make a significant contribution to understanding Irish society in the past. Together with thirty-four earlier works in this series they explore something of the hopes and fears of those who lived in Irish local communities in the past. In doing so they provide examples of the practice of local history at its best and show the vibrant discipline which the study of local history in Ireland has become in recent years.

Maynooth Studies in Irish Local History: Number 37

In Search of Thomas Sheahan: Radical Politics in Cork, 1824–36

Fintan Lane

IRISH ACADEMIC PRESS
DUBLIN • PORTLAND, OR

First published in 2001 by
IRISH ACADEMIC PRESS
44, Northumberland Road, Dublin 4, Ireland
and in the United States of America by
IRISH ACADEMIC PRESS
c/o ISBS, 5824 NE Hassalo Street, Portland, OR 97213–3644.

website: www.iap.ie

British Library Cataloguing in Publication Data
Lane, Fintan
   In search of Thomas Sheahan: radical politics in Cork, 1824–1836. – (Maynooth
   studies in Irish local history; no. 37)
   1. Sheahan, Thomas   2. Politicians – Ireland – Cork – Biography   3. Radicalism
   – Ireland – Cork – History – 19th century   4. Cork (Ireland) – Politics and
   government – 19th century
   I. Title
   941.9'56'081
   ISBN 0–7165–2742–1

A catalog record of this book is available from the Library of Congress.

Typeset in 10 pt on 12 pt Bembo by
Carrigboy Typesetting Services, County Cork
Printed by Creative Print and Design (Wales) Ebbw Vale

Contents

Acknowledgements

My thanks are due to a number of people and institutions who assisted me in various ways during the course of my research: the staff of the National Library of Ireland, the National Archives of Ireland, the British Library, the British Newspaper Library (at Colindale), the National Library of Australia (which, remarkably, proved to be the most accessible repository of Sheahan's 1834 pamphlet), the Cork Archives Institute, the Boole Library at University College Cork, the library of the University of Limerick, the Cork City Library, and the Cork County Library.

I would similarly like to extend my thanks to Joe Guerin who read and commented on an early draft of this work. I owe a particular debt to Andy Bielenberg whose extensive knowledge of Cork's industrial history was put at my disposal. Andy's detailed reading of the penultimate draft encouraged a number of useful alterations, although as the stock phrase puts it neither he nor Joe should be held responsible for my interpretations or for any errors of fact if such exist.

Introduction

In the opinion of Irish historiography, grandiloquent as it sounds, Daniel O'Connell bestrides the 1820s and 1830s like a Colossus.[1] This local study, however, is primarily concerned with the multifarious nature and complex effects of the movements which O'Connell dominated, and it seeks to illuminate the activity of organised tradesmen in Cork city. Thomas Sheahan, whose political career forms the core of this study, was an influential local leader of the radical wing of O'Connellism and his active involvement between 1824 and 1836 neatly coincides with the rise of that movement. A newspaper editor, pamphleteer, political agitator, and social reformer he viewed himself as working class by birth and in his political discourse he stressed that his central priority was the plight of the poor rather than the promotion of a new political elite.

After Sheahan's death in March 1836 the Cork Trades Association, which he founded, built a substantial monument to his memory in St. Joseph's cemetery on the southside of Cork city (fig. 1). The inscriptions, unusually for the time, are in Ogham, Irish and English and they attest to the respect and affection felt for Sheahan. The epithet in English reads:

> He was an accomplished scholar and a practical Christian. Disinterested in his views and gentle in his manners. But when roused by public wrong and, above all, by the oppression of the poor, to whose welfare his whole heart was devoted, his spirit was fearless and uncompromising. A rare example how much may be effected for freedom and humanity by the energies and virtue of an individual even when unaided by the accident of wealth or high station.

In 1839 John Windele, the well-known Cork antiquarian, praised Sheahan for his 'bold and uncompromising advocacy of popular rights ... and in particular those of the operative or working classes,' but, in addition, Windele remembered him as 'a man above faction, and a scrupulous and unbending lover of truth and justice'.[2] Opinions differed regarding the extent of Sheahan's generosity towards his political rivals but he did enjoy widespread respect in O'Connellite Cork.

The 1820s and 1830s were decades of great change in Ireland. The late 1820s witnessed a massive struggle for Catholic emancipation and the emergence of a democracy movement enjoying strong support from the working class.[3] In January 1824 the Catholic Association had reduced its membership fee from one-guinea-a-year to one-penny-a-month thus facilitating

1. Monument to Sheahan, St Joseph's cemetery, erected by
Cork Trades Association in 1836

the transformation of itself from a solidly middle class pressure group into a widely supported movement embracing all classes of Catholics in Ireland. Within five years this movement achieved a measure of success, including the right of Catholics to sit in parliament, although the gains were circumscribed by a continued distinction between Catholic and Protestant subjects and by O'Connell's willingness to sacrifice the franchise of the forty-shilling freeholders on the altar of political expediency.[4]

The 1830s was a decade of reform and change in both Britain and Ireland in terms of the parliamentary franchise, the treatment of the destitute, and official attitudes to the trade union movement. Ireland, moreover, began the decade with boisterous socio-political mobilisations demanding the abolition of tithes and the repeal of the Act of Union with Britain. The success of the movement for Catholic emancipation infused confidence in the rising Catholic middle class and its liberal Protestant allies. The exclusion of the Tories from government throughout most of the 1830s added hope to the aspirations of many Irish radicals. Sheahan was one of those who formed the local cadre in these campaigns for social and political reform. His story allows us an insight into pre-Famine nationalist and liberal politics, and their effects at local level, but it also further alerts us to the dangers of seeing homogeneity in movements that were essentially composed of disparate elements.

My initial interest in Thomas Sheahan arose from a lazy amble through a graveyard. Faded monuments to the Catholic merchants of nineteenth-century Cork can be seen throughout St Joseph's cemetery in the Ballyphehane district of Cork city. Buried alongside these pillars of past commerce are several social and political activists from the same period. During a grave-spotting stroll on a rather murky September morning I came across the burial sites of Fr Theobold Mathew (the anti-alcohol campaigner), Charles Sugrue (a merchant and active Repealer), Eugene Crean (a home rule MP), Charles Guilfoyle Doran and Cornelius P. O'Sullivan (both important Fenian leaders). None of these, however, had a memorial that could vie with that which I discovered behind the rear-wall of the inner cemetery. Sheahan's four-columned neoclassical monument is remarkable for its grandeur but also for its multi-lingual and effusive epithet. Moreover, I had never heard of Thomas Sheahan and knew little of the Cork Trades Association that inscribed its praise for the edification of future amblers.

This short study is an attempt to understand Sheahan and the *milieu* that he and his associates inhabited. In the first chapter what is known of his early life is documented and his entry into political activity is explored. The second chapter examines his role as newspaper editor and political activist during the late 1820s. The later chapters consider Sheahan at the height of his influence from 1832 to his premature death at the age of thirty-nine. Thomas Sheahan can only be understood in conjunction with the Cork working class and, consequently, its story is central to this pamphlet.

Early years

Thomas Sheahan was born in 1797 to Thomas and Catherine Sheahan in a working class district on the northside of Cork city.[1] References to his family background are rare but it is clear that it was not especially affluent and Sheahan himself on a number of occasions stressed his working-class origins. In late 1833, in an address to tradesmen, he reminded his readers that he was 'the son, and the grandson, and the nephew, and the cousin of tradesmen and journeymen' while in evidence submitted to the Irish poor inquiry of 1834 he stated that he was the son of 'humble parents' and that his relatives were, 'for the most part of the working classes'.[2]

Sheahan's family lived in the Shandon Street area and was certainly working class in origin but while his father was a carpenter, probably a coffin-maker, he also had his own business and in socio-economic terms the Sheahans could most accurately be categorised as lower middle class.[3] The Sheahans were undertakers and suppliers of funeral accessories with a residence and business premises in Dominick Street (formerly known as Shandon Castle Lane) which was substantial enough to entitle Thomas Sheahan senior to the franchise as a £20 freeholder.[4] The family lived in that section of Dominick Street which runs between Shandon Street and the Butter Exchange and, except for brief periods, Thomas lived in this street throughout his life. 'My residence,' he accurately declared in 1834, 'has been in the vicinity of great poverty [and] my mind, at all times, both previously to and during my connexion with the press, turned on the distressed condition of those about me'.[5]

During his early years fever, dysentery and disease were regular visitors to the densely inhabited alleys and laneways adjoining Dominick Street. Indeed, at the end of 1797 there was a particularly bad outbreak of fever, which was widely attributed to the poor sanitary and living conditions in the overcrowded houses.[6] There can be no doubt that Sheahan's childhood in this area was a formative influence on his *mentalité*, and his continued residence made it impossible to disregard the socio-economic destitution that pervaded many working-class districts in the city. In January 1817, at a time of extreme hardship, a census of the pauper population of Cork provided a grim picture (table 1).[7]

In three of these returns only the number of individuals was stated while only the families were recorded in the parish of St Paul's. If we accept that the figure for individuals in that parish was roughly 2,600 then the total number of paupers in Cork city in 1817 amounted to some 20,815 or approximately 25 per cent of the population. Again, during the crisis of 1822 a survey

Table 1. Census of Cork paupers, 1817

Parishes	No. of families pauperised	No. of individuals who are paupers
St Anne's, Shandon	–	4,130
St Mary's, Shandon	574	2,364
St Nicholas	919	3,979
St Peter's	–	2,176
St Paul's	660	–
Holy Trinity	–	2,029
St Finbarr's	786	3,537

Source: *Southern Reporter* 29 August 1826; *Cork Constitution* 31 August 1826.

indicated those in distress ('unemployed and starving') amounted to 20,136 in a city population of 80,114, and of those in distress 10,805 lived in the two Shandon parishes.[8]

Dominick Street, however, was also close to the heart of an extremely important commercial area. The Cork Butter Market, which had been formalised in 1769, operated primarily from the Shandon (or North) weighhouse which was less than a few hundred yards from where the Sheahans lived. Dominick Street itself contained the premises of as many as seven butter merchants according to an 1824 directory.[9] In the early 1800s, while other Cork industries waned, the butter trade continued to prosper providing consistent employment for a section of the coopering trade.[10] When Thomas Sheahan was a child the weighmaster at the nearby butter market was a Protestant unionist and militiaman called Thomas Ring. It seems unlikely that the Catholic Sheahans had any social contact with the Ring family but in later years one of Thomas Ring's sons, William (born in 1796), became a key ally and friend of Sheahan in the Cork Trades Association.

Little is known of Sheahan's life up to 1823 except that he trained for several years for the Catholic priesthood.[11] The creation of Maynooth College by an act of parliament in 1795 made it more feasible for somebody from his social background to aspire to the priesthood. Indeed, it has often been argued that the arrival of the Maynooth seminary prompted the emergence of a new clergy with humbler social origins and stronger political attitudes.[12] Before Maynooth those who wished to train for the priesthood often travelled to continental seminaries and this could involve considerable expense for the family of the aspirant. However, S.J. Connolly has argued that the removal of this impediment did not lead to a deluge of poor working-class applicants. The sons of tradesmen and small shopkeepers, like Sheahan, continued to form the lowest social layer within the priesthood.[13]

Sheahan remained devoutly religious throughout his life but he failed to complete his clerical training and returned to Cork in the early 1820s. It is unclear why he abandoned his studies although in 1836 the *Southern Reporter* newspaper attributed his decision to a desire to openly involve himself in political life on behalf of the poor.[14] However, this is unlikely to have been the reason as opportunities for Catholics to involve themselves in local and national politics were virtually non-existent before the rise of the movement for Catholic emancipation.

With a good education Thomas Sheahan was able to seek work as a private tutor. In 1823 he secured a position with the family of Rickard Deasy and moved to live at their home in Mill Street in the west Cork town of Clonakilty.[15] The Deasys, somewhat like the O'Connells of Derrynane, were Catholics who were reputed to have made their fortune from the widespread smuggling that occurred along the southern coast during the eighteenth century. Indeed, one local historian has claimed that these two smuggling families were closely linked and sometimes engaged in joint operations.[16] By the early nineteenth century the Deasys had established themselves as successful brewers and were considered one of the most influential Catholic commercial families in west Cork. More importantly, in terms of Sheahan's political development, Rickard Deasy was a staunch liberal with an active interest in the growing demand for Catholic emancipation.

Ireland suffered a partial famine in 1821–2 and issues such as tithes, land rents and (to a lesser degree) landlord absenteeism were causes of popular discontent. However, the primary issue for the rising Catholic middle class at the beginning of the 1820s was its continued exclusion from the polity and from a variety of legal, civic and military positions. Those like Rickard Deasy who already held economic power resented their exclusion from political power. In a country that was 80 per cent Catholic these legal restrictions, such as the inability of Catholics to sit in parliament, were seen as manifestly unjust and the demand for greater democracy enjoyed wide support. An important new departure in the struggle for emancipation occurred in May 1823 while Sheahan was ensconced in the Deasy household. In Dublin a Catholic Association was founded with the intention of using all constitutional means to win the lifting of restrictions on Catholics in Ireland. Initially, the yearly subscription of £1 1s. meant that membership was entirely restricted to the nobility and middle class but from the outset some leading figures pushed for a more vigorous approach to agitation.

Daniel O'Connell, a prominent lawyer from Kerry, soon emerged as the driving force and in late May he argued that the Catholic Association should mobilise support by taking up the 'many grievances under which the poor and unprotected Catholic peasant smarted' by demanding redress through parliamentary measures even before the granting of Catholic emancipation.[17] Tithes and church rates were foremost among the grievances that he identified.

In June O'Connell spoke again of the 'wretched, naked, persecuted peasant' and he threatened to persuade the Catholics of Ireland 'to act with the Reformers of England'.[18] With these populist verbal gestures O'Connell helped to raise expectations regarding what could be achieved through the struggle for Catholic emancipation and he began to widen the support-base of his middle class pressure group.

The most important event in the development of the Catholic Association was the reduction on 24 January 1824 of its subscription fee. O'Connell won approval for a reduction to 1*d*. per month for associate members with the intention of raising subscriptions in every parish in the country. His scheme for collecting what became known as the 'Catholic rent' involved the appointment of a treasurer, secretary and committee in each county and by June almost 200,000 copies of the 'rent plan' and 4,000 collector's books were in circulation.[19] The 'rent' was meant to serve as a barometer of public opinion towards emancipation and, naturally, as a mechanism for funding the campaign. In practise it led to a mass mobilisation in support of O'Connell's demands for constitutional change.

The collection of the 'rent' went slowly in its initial weeks but by April it began to gather pace with the urban areas among the first to organise. In Clonakilty a parochial meeting, chaired by Rickard Deasy, was held in late April and Thomas Sheahan acted as secretary.[20] Sheahan had already begun to show some interest in political life and was a regular attendee at the Clonakilty petty sessions court where he was appalled by the behaviour of the magistrates. In early 1824, under the signature of 'An Observer', he had several letters published in the *Southern Reporter* complaining of their conduct in the case of four local men who were ordered to be transferred to Cork city for trial under the Insurrection Act. In the event Sheahan's qualms were proved to be justified when the prisoners were subsequently acquitted.[21] To the annoyance of the local ultra-unionist element he continued to report on the work of the Clonakilty court. His involvement as secretary of the first Catholic parochial meeting caused further irritation and the unionist *Cork Advertiser* attacked him in early May for both attending the petty sessions as a reporter (and thus being a troublemaker) and for allegedly being a stooge of his employer Rickard Deasy.[22]

This episode marks Sheahan's entrance into public life and he responded in the self-confident and strident manner that became a consistent feature of his political behaviour. A hostile observer later remarked that Sheahan's muscular physique and his equally muscular opinions 'would at once convince you that he was one not easily to be met'.[23] In a letter to the pro-Catholic *Cork Mercantile Chronicle* he admitted that he was in Deasy's employment but he declared that he did not consider himself a dependent, or unable to survive without Deasy. 'I lived', he wrote, 'independently of every man, except my father, before I had the pleasure of entering Mr. Deasy's house' and when he left he would do so again. He attacked the *Advertiser*'s correlation of wealth and 'respectability' and he asserted that he 'would leave no stone unturned in order to make the practice of reporting the proceedings of such Courts as that of Clonakilty general throughout Ireland . . . If any Irish Magistrate could be silly enough to rise against the publicity of his conduct, the motive would be obvious, and the voice and practice of England would crush him'.[24] His residual faith in English justice is evident in this letter, as is his conviction that public exposure could bring relief. 'I had my reward', he wrote in 1833, 'in the blessings of many a poor man who felt that in the publicity . . . lay much of his protection against oppression'.[25] In fact, in his 1824 reportage of the Clonakilty petty sessions court Sheahan was something of a journalistic innovator as such reports had yet to become common in Irish newspapers.

Sheahan maintained his involvement in the expanding Catholic emancipation movement and he appears to have attended public meetings in other parts of west Cork.[26] However, he also developed an interest in political journalism and in June 1824 the *Cork Mercantile Chronicle* published the first section of a three-part satirical play, titled 'Mirror of Justice', in which he assailed the tithe system. The subsequent two parts poked fun at the local judicial system, the landlords and a recent influx of bible proselytisers.[27] In October the newspaper printed a long letter in which he argued for an organised approach to the next general election by those who wanted social and political change in Ireland. This letter is especially interesting because it shows that Sheahan felt that the abolition of the tithe system, which was the subject of an ongoing agitation, was as crucial an issue as Catholic emancipation itself. He condemned those pro-emancipation members of parliament who supported the tithes and argued that the presence of such MPs in London helped to convince the English public that there was considerable support for the tithe system in Ireland. In general he was unimpressed by the Irish MPs:

> There is not a representative from Ireland . . . who is not more or less intimately identified with the grievances of that land. Take a survey of them all, and you cannot name a single individual among them who has not some near relative or friend fattening on the Church Establishment, the Ascendancy principle, the Rackrent system, Absenteeism, or Taxation.[28]

He suggested that in order to return MPs who would oppose tithes, judicial corruption, rack-renting, and support Catholic emancipation, it was necessary to mobilise voters on a parish-by-parish basis.

Moreover, he firmly believed that the poorer voters could be broken from landlord influence: 'They feel that they belong to a people ground down and trodden'.[29] However, to induce these voters to elect their 'friends' rather than their 'enemies' Sheahan argued that it was necessary to create a sense of communal solidarity.

First – An Aggregate Meeting of the People of Ireland, to be held in Dublin, for the purpose of recommending to those having votes, the appointment of honest and intelligent men.

Secondly – Aggregate Meetings of each County and City, for recommending particular candidates.

Thirdly – Parochial Meetings for the same purpose.

Fourthly – The distribution of 400,000 circulars, shewing forth clearly and forcibly, the advantages that would result to the Country from sending honest men to the British Parliament, and most particularly, at the present moment.[30]

Sheahan's faith in the forty-shilling freeholders was not shared by many in the leadership of the Catholic Association, although the *Dublin Evening Post* had been arguing since August that this category of voter should be seen as a latent force for change.[31] Daniel O'Connell was not convinced of their value and when an election finally arrived in 1826 any successes were the result of local initiatives, such as in Waterford, and not due to any national organisation by the Catholic Association. In fact, it was Thomas Wyse of Waterford, and not O'Connell, who set about creating a national electoral machine from the emancipation movement. Wyse, like Sheahan, stressed the importance of involving the poorer classes in constitutional politics.[32]

By the end of 1824 Thomas Sheahan had left Deasy's employment. In 1825 he travelled to London where he spent most of that year, possibly as a journalist or seeking work in journalism.[33] Daniel O'Connell likewise went to London in February 1825 and he remained there until May lobbying for Catholic emancipation and learning the nuances of English politics.[34] Sheahan attended a number of meetings in London at which O'Connell spoke.[35] More interestingly, he wrote a short book, essentially a political travelogue, entitled *Excursions from Bandon* that was published by the prestigious firm, Longman and partners, of Paternoster Row. This was a clever, well-written and interesting examination of Irish grievances aimed primarily at English readers. In order to encourage empathy from his projected audience Sheahan constructed 'a plain Englishman', or rather a slack-jawed English liberal, as the supposed writer of the book. The author purportedly developed an interest in Irish affairs as a result of a chance encounter with an Irishman some years earlier and in the summer of 1824 a business trip to west Cork allowed him to devote some time to acquiring a personal knowledge of the country. 'I said to myself,' he writes, 'that I should see if the discontents and poverty of its people arose from themselves or from bad treatment'.[36]

Excursions from Bandon was entirely intended as a piece of political propaganda but Sheahan displayed a fluid prose style and he often employed elaborate descriptive detail in order to buttress the authorial pretence. It was a very readable book. Drawing on his time with the Deasys, Sheahan places his

Englishman in Bandon and has him make several trips to explore the surrounding countryside in the direction of Ballineen, the Muskery mountains, Clonakilty and Timoleague. He points out that although an English speaker could generally be found these districts were largely Irish-speaking and 'seven-tenths . . . knew none other than their native tongue'.[37] This clearly was not a problem for Sheahan who was himself an Irish speaker but it did serve to underline the otherness of Ireland on a cultural as well as a political level. The Englishman's first detailed conversation on Irish matters is held with a varied group of Catholics, Episcopalians and Dissenters in the Shannon Arms Inn at Bandon. Arguments are presented in favour of Catholic emancipation and the abolition of tithes, and against the treatment of tenants by bad landlords, landlord absenteeism, the conduct of Irish magistrates, the grand-jury system and the debilitating 'want of trade'.[38] These themes, along with some others, are pursued at greater length throughout the rest of text as the Englishman encounters individuals and circumstances that bring him to an understanding of the depth of 'monopoly, injustice, and inhumanity in Ireland'.[39]

The book allows us an insight into Sheahan's position on a number of important issues. He lambasted the legal restrictions on Catholics and described the penal laws as an attempt to 'starve the Catholics into Protestantism' but he opposed religious sectarianism and asserted that they 'should distinguish the good man from the bad system with which he may be connected'. While supporting the disestablishment of the Church of Ireland he described the Protestant clergy as 'a moral, a learned, and a highly respectable body of men'.[40] This characterisation differed markedly from some comments addressed to a Cork readership the previous year when he had spoken of the 'oppressive parson' stripping 'the flesh from the bone' of the Catholic peasant.[41] The sectarian division between Catholic and Protestant was an important feature of political life in the 1820s and Sheahan, like many others, could use rhetoric that was intended as political criticism but seen as something else by those who feared the rise of the Catholic democracy. His opposition was to the Protestant monopoly of political power and, more specifically, to the tithe system whereby the majority population had to contribute financially to the established church to which they did not belong.

'The Catholics,' he wrote, 'fight the battles of the Empire, and pay taxes, still they are degraded'. Sheahan admitted that the Protestants of England considered it dangerous to trust the Catholic with political power but in terms of taxes and the tithes he reasoned that it was manifestly unfair to expect a person 'who is blackballed out of a club' to 'pay the entrance fees'.[42] Three years later he employed the lexicon of the American revolution when he described this policy as one of opposition to taxation without representation.[43] He believed that these arguments would make more immediate headway in England than the stark demand for Catholic emancipation. In other words, Irish reformers should first concentrate on the abolition of tithes: 'The Irish Catholics are more likely to gain ground with the English Protestants by complaining of pecuniary privation than of exclusion from political power'.[44]

However, he saw a distinct link between social gains, such as the abolition of tithes or the provision of education, and eventual political emancipation. One would lead to the other: 'Let the domestic comforts of the peasant be encreased, and let him continue unemancipated, that is degraded, without diminishing his discontent, you but supply him with the means of resistance'. And again:

> It will be readily admitted, that if the people of Ireland were com-
> fortable and educated, for education is the rage of all, insurrections
> would be more rare; but the spirit of discontent would not be the less
> active or efficient. Political inferiority would be the never-failing
> excitement to commotion. Improved means would supply the materials
> for attack, and education would give them a scientific direction.[45]

Sheahan was arguing that the struggles for social improvement and political emancipation were in fact the same struggle. 'The oppression practised by landlords, and agents, and corporators and the rest,' he wrote, 'is a necessary adjunct to political exclusion'.[46]

His book also visited the Clonakilty petty sessions court and he inserted himself in this scene as a reporter whom the magistrates would like to expel from the building. The Englishman is informed that because 'all the minutiae of the tythe and toll systems, of rackrenting, of charges against the police, gentlefolks and the like, came before the magistrate' there was a fear of public exposure. Again, Sheahan was highlighting his belief in the power of the press and, indeed, newspapers did play a crucial role in the development of the emancipation movement.[47]

Another target of *Excursions from Bandon* was the 'enormous evil' of landlord absenteeism that he, interestingly, linked to unemployment among tradesmen because of the wealth that was extracted from the country instead of invested in the manufacturing sector. Modern historians have criticised this argument on the contended assumption that there was no substantive economic difference between ordinary rent and absentee rent because both often involved the transfer of potential capital out of Ireland.[48] The appendices to the book included an address from the cotton manufacturers of Cork blaming problems in the industry on 'want of capital.' Another appendix, as a criticism of the import trade, gave the statistics for ships and tonnage that entered Irish ports in 1824.[49] In general, however, the problems of urban Ireland did not loom large in Sheahan's first book.

By the end of 1825 it is clear that Thomas Sheahan had begun to establish a reputation for himself in his native Cork. He had exposed the magistrates of Clonakilty, stood up to an attack from the unionist press, played an honourable

role in the struggle for Catholic emancipation, written political satire
attacking the tithes and the landlords, and had published a book in London
that cogently articulated Irish grievances. *Excursions from Bandon* was probably
the achievement that persuaded John Pearce, the proprietor of the pro-
Catholic and liberal *Cork Mercantile Chronicle*, to offer Sheahan the editorship
of this newspaper despite his limited experience in journalism. Sheahan, not
surprisingly, accepted Pearce's offer and moved back to Cork.

Demanding democracy

Thomas Sheahan took up his new post as editor of the *Cork Mercantile Chronicle* in January 1826 and he returned to live with his parents in Dominick Street.[1] His arrival at the *Chronicle* offices at 12 Patrick Street coincided with a strike by the journeymen tailors of Cork for the maintenance of the 3s. 6d. per day, which they had received since 1810.[2] Similarly, both the operative cabinet-makers and the shoemakers struck in January against wage-cuts and in April carpenters in the harbour town of Cove also went out demanding a rate of 3s. 4d. per day.[3] This wave of militancy was sparked off by the assimilation of the Irish and the English currencies which caused a wage reduction of 1d. in every shilling.

In general, however, 1826 was marked less by labour disputes and more by severe unemployment and social destitution. The woollen and cotton weavers were worst hit by the economic downturn and by June more than two hundred in Cork city were forced into breaking stones for an allowance of just 1s. per day. The weavers were outraged in mid-June when an alleged lack of funds threatened to reduce this 'entirely inadequate' wage.[4] A similar reduction in Dublin led to an angry demonstration by distressed weavers outside the Royal Exchange on 12 July, and in August the *Chronicle* reported food riots in the capital city.[5] The mayor of Cork, Thomas Harrison of Tivoli Terrace, wrote some weeks later to the lord lieutenant asking that the government establish 'public works' to alleviate the crisis but a letter in early September from Henry Goulburn of Dublin Castle refused this request although £200 was forwarded to add to the local distress fund.[6]

The distress in Cork city and the clearly deficient response by the authorities prompted a series of public meetings at which the introduction to Ireland of a system of poor laws was discussed. These meetings, which Sheahan attended, were highly animated with many local shopkeepers and merchants opposing the imposition of such laws. Gerard Callaghan, unionist scion of one of the city's richest families, encapsulated the Tory position when he argued in August 1826 that he did not 'know that there was any written authority – any dictum of jurist, asserting the rights of able-bodied men, if destitute, to public provision'.[7] Opposition was mainly focused on the issue of increased taxes, although economic arguments were occasionally employed. *The Constitution*, the organ of Cork unionism, protested that a 'permanent' system of relief was 'calculated to destroy industry, foresight, and economy in the poor; to extinguish compassion in the rich; and by destroying the demand for and the supply of labour, to spread a degraded population over a ruined land'.[8] The newspaper encouraged a series of meetings aimed at undermining a petition supporting poor laws which had been sent from Cork to the London government. In Dublin the *Freeman's Journal* was critical of some of Gerard Callaghan's views but it did concur with him in agreeing that the poor had no 'right' to be 'supported by the rest of the community'.[9]

Sheahan was strongly in favour of the introduction of legal provisions for the poor and he used the *Chronicle* to promote his position: 'Do we not know that, in the present involved and artificial state of society, a man may be industrious, skilful, and sober, and still incapable of supporting nature. Is that man to starve?'[10] In September 1826 at a public meeting in the vestry-room of St Mary's parish he spoke, according to *The Constitution*, 'with considerable effect' in favour of the introduction of poor laws to Ireland.[11] Initially, at this meeting he was denied the right to speak because he was not a householder but his residence in the area and, most importantly, the fact that his father was a ratepayer won him a hearing. In 1829 in a lengthy paper published in the *Irish Catholic Magazine* Sheahan insisted that even those who were destitute through their own improvidence should be entitled to aid under a poor law system.[12] Again, in 1834 he wrote that in the event of social destitution he believed that 'men should not be allowed to want – that the property of the community should be available to them, and – of right'.[13]

One of the most interesting contributions to the Cork debates of 1826 was that of William Thompson, the socialist philosopher. Thompson, who lived at 4 Patrick Street (close to the *Chronicle* office), was a retired merchant and landowner from a wealthy local Protestant family.[14] At a public meeting on 22 August he made a detailed speech in favour of establishing co-operative communities in the vicinity of Cork city as a way of dealing with urban destitution. He condemned the English poor laws and cited London tradesmen as critics of the system.[15] In proposing his alternative plan he stressed that he was suggesting a scheme for the permanent relief of the unemployed poor 'in the most beneficial manner to themselves, and if possible without compulsory taxation'.[16] The reference to taxation was clearly a lure to interest the more avaricious in the scheme but in the event little support materialised. Dolores Dooley has noted an increased urgency from September 1826 in Thompson's plans for the establishment of actual co-operative communities.[17] It is clear that this sense of urgency derived directly from his experiences in his native city during the preceding months.

In the winter of 1822–3 Thompson's colleague, Robert Owen, had toured Ireland in a similar attempt to interest the nobility and middle class in the idea of co-operatives as a social panacea but he had likewise encountered limited interest.[18] Thompson's scheme was not taken very seriously and the idea of Irish poor laws was merely notional in 1826. Such laws were not introduced into Ireland until 1838. As was usual in instances of extreme destitution a fund was established to alleviate the distress and Sheahan was among the first to subscribe contributing the not inconsiderable sum of £2.[19]

Cork in the 1820s was a city split as much on politico-religious grounds as on those of class. Indeed, John B. O'Brien has accurately argued that the local political battleground was dominated by politico-religious rivals, most of whom were members of the city's divided middle class.[20] It would be too simple to describe the political scene in terms of Catholics versus Protestants but there is a rough reality to that picture. Class antagonisms did exist, as evidenced by the activities of trade unionists throughout the 1820s, but the struggle against the Protestant monopoly of political power united Catholics across all social classes. However, in the campaign for Catholic emancipation and especially in the campaign for the reform of municipal government it was the Catholic middle class which was to the forefront, with the aid of a small number of liberal Protestants such as the Crawfords and the Beamishs. The working class was much less interested than it was in the later demand for the repeal of the Act of Union. One of the reasons for this can be found in the property-based nature of the franchise and the limited gains that workers expected from such reforms.

The population of Cork city in the late 1820s was approximately 84,000 with another 22,000 living in the liberties within the parliamentary constituency of the 'County of the City of Cork'.[21] The 1834 religious census showed roughly 77,500 Catholics, 15,500 members of the Church of Ireland, 384 Presbyterians, and 780 assorted Methodists, Quakers, Unitarians and other Protestant dissenters.[22] These figures are rather imprecise but they do indicate that members of the established church (those in the Church of Ireland) made up less than 17 per cent of the population yet they controlled the institutions of local government from which Catholics were excluded. Municipal politics was monopolised by a group of local Protestant families who organised themselves in a powerful clique known as the Friendly Club.[23] This club was especially involved in the selection of mayors, sheriffs and other municipal officers. Among the most prominent of these families were the Besnards, Lanes, Perriers and Newsoms but there were others who joined in order to gain access to the corporation's extensive sphere of influence. The Friendly Club, which was staunchly Tory and virulently against emancipation, was hated by the city's Catholic middle class and Thomas Sheahan shared this distaste. As editor of the strongly pro-Catholic *Cork Mercantile Chronicle* he consistently demanded municipal reform and harshly criticised the corporation at every opportunity.

Only freemen were eligible to be members of Cork corporation which, in addition to giving the Tory element control of local political power, allowed the manipulation of the parliamentary electoral register. Voters were either 'freeholders' or 'freemen'.[24] The freeholders gained the vote through a property qualification and were predominantly Catholic while the freemen,

including non-residents, were elected by the common council of the corporation and were predominantly Protestant. A self-perpetuating system was
established through which the mayor, sheriff and the aldermen selected the
freemen who in turn elected the members of the corporation. Of 2,665
freemen in 1833, for example, only seventy-three were Catholics.[25] In fact,
between 1825 and a government investigation in 1833 not a single Catholic
freeman was elected by the corporation.

The Catholic middle class responded to this Protestant monopoly by
establishing a Chamber of Commerce in 1819. Affluent Catholic merchants
and manufacturers dominated the Cork Chamber of Commerce although it
was explicitly non-sectarian and also included many of the city's most
prominent liberal Protestants. The Chamber's rooms (which also encompassed
a hotel) at 104 Patrick Street were the locus of planning and plotting by pro-
emancipationists and, despite protestations of apoliticism, they were a hive of
political activity throughout the 1820s and 1830s. Sheahan soon orientated
himself towards this powerful political faction whose leading figures included
Daniel Meagher, a successful wine and spirits merchant, Joseph Hayes, a
distiller in the Glen, Thomas Lyons, a woollen manufacturer, Charles Sugrue,
a general merchant, William Fagan, a butter merchant, and other wealthy
Catholics. Dan Meagher and his friends were the embodiment of moderation
but they were indefatigable in their opposition to the political monopoly
exercised by their Protestant economic equals.

Protestants, because of the 'freeman' system, formed the majority of parliamentary voters in Cork city but, even before the franchise reform of 1832, the
mainly Catholic freeholders often found that they could exert significant
influence at elections. By the late 1820s the number of Catholic voters had
increased with the continuous addition of new forty-shilling freeholders.
Moreover, the Catholics sometimes found themselves holding the balance of
power at election-time because of divisions within the Protestant camp. The
non-resident freemen were inclined more towards the aristocratic and landlord
interest rather than the city merchant interest and in the elections of 1818 and
1820 this meant that the Catholic freeholders were able to successfully weigh the
balance in favour of Christopher Hely-Hutchinson, a substantial landowner,
brother of the earl of Donoughmore, and pro-emancipation Whig.[26] Added,
of course, to the Catholic vote and the landed interest were the votes of liberal
city businessmen like William Thompson and the Beamishes.

With the development of the movement for Catholic emancipation the
Catholic middle class began to play a more active and organised role in
parliamentary elections. Dan Meagher, with the assistance of Sheahan as editor
of the *Chronicle*, was central to this heightened involvement in the late 1820s.
At the end of August 1826 Christopher Hely-Hutchinson MP died in
England precipitating a contest for his seat that saw Gerard Callaghan emerge
as a pro-Tory candidate and John Hely-Hutchinson, a son of the dead MP, as

a pro-emancipation Liberal candidate.[27] Callaghan was in many senses the *bête noire* of Catholic Cork during the 1820s and early 1830s because of his pronounced conservatism and his religious apostasy. His father, Daniel Callaghan, was a Catholic merchant and contractor who had developed a prosperous business during the American war and the Anglo-French conflict. The Callaghans owned land as well as one of the largest distilleries in Cork city.[28] Sheahan somewhat understated the position when he later observed that the 'influence of the Callaghan family was unquestionably great' in late 1820s Cork.[29]

Gerard Callaghan's politics, especially his negative attitude to the emancipation movement, were the primary reason for opposition to his candidature in 1826 but underlying this was a strongly held prejudice against his conversion to Protestantism and a well-founded belief that he was fundamentally opportunistic and self-interested. However, Callaghan was politically adept and by the late 1820s he succeeded in uniting the urban and county Protestant Tory vote against the perceived threat of Catholic emancipation.[30] Sheahan argued that Hely-Hutchinson should be supported against Callaghan because of the latters championing of the system 'by which the race from which he was sprung had been long ... trampled in the dust' and, in addition, he confessed that he 'could discern nothing but ambition in the man'.[31]

In a satirical piece that Sheahan wrote for the *Chronicle* in early December he lampooned Callaghan, whom he nicknamed 'Janus', and accused him of still being a Catholic when he obtained his freeholder franchise in 1812.[32] The import of this allegation was that it contradicted Callaghan's claim to have converted to the established church while at school in England and thus rendered him a liar. In the event, at the close of the poll on 27 December 1826, Hely-Hutchinson narrowly won the seat with 1,019 votes against 970 for Callaghan. The Liberals were clearly satisfied with Callaghan's defeat but, as Sheahan later remarked, the fact that Hely-Hutchinson had expended £15,500 during the campaign pointed to the continued existence of vote-buying and electoral corruption on all sides.[33] The poll book for the election records a 'Thomas Sheehan' of 'Shandon Castle Lane' (Dominick Street) among those who voted for Hely-Hutchinson – this was almost certainly Sheahan's father who was still alive at that time.[34] Sheahan himself, as a mere boarder in his parent's house, did not have a vote and in fact it was 1832 before he acquired the franchise.[35]

Those who had most prominently supported Hely-Hutchinson were, by and large, connected to the Chamber of Commerce and they included the group (Meagher, Lyons, Sugrue, Jeremiah Murphy, and others) who had established the city committee of the Catholic Association at a meeting in Carey's Lane in early April 1824.[36] The Clonakilty meeting, at which Sheahan had acted as secretary, was held later in that month and other county towns soon organised similar meetings. Cork city and county contributed the largest amount in the first phase (ending March 1825) of the 'Catholic rent' collection.[37] The Catholic Association in Cork city, especially because of the Chamber of Commerce, retained a strong sense of cohesion despite the formal suppression of the organisation in March 1825. In early January 1827, following their victory over Callaghan, this group organised a meeting to promote the registration of freeholders in order to increase the Liberal influence in future elections.[38] In general, the Catholic emancipationists did little during January and February 1827 but Cork did not share this national quiescence and more than twenty town and parochial Catholic meetings were held across the county.[39] This flurry of activity was directly related to the contested election of December 1826.

In April an 'aggregate meeting' was convened in the South Parish Catholic church and Daniel O'Connell was among the 5,000 who attended. A resolution was adopted calling for the drawing up of a petition to be sent to the London parliament demanding emancipation: 'a full, free, and entire representation of the people of this island in the Commons House of Parliament'. Another resolution, proposed by the distiller James Daly, denounced the compulsory payment of Church of Ireland clergymen by the Catholic taxpayers. Nonetheless, the rest of 1827 was something of a lacuna for the emancipation movement and Sheahan, who had helped to organise the April meeting, complained in August 1828 that little had been done since: 'Not a single petition has gone forth from your City or County . . . We find persons enough to speak; but few to do the work'.[40]

Interestingly, in December 1827 a forum for discussion emerged in Cork with the opening of the Lyceum by Thomas Shinkwin. This new venue, which was a revival of an older debating society, probably held little appeal for Sheahan, and John Boyle of *The Freeholder* portrayed it negatively:

> Well then December four, the talkers came,
> Both high and low, with and without a name;
> James Daly, esquire, Messieurs Walsh and Barry,
> Murphy, McCarthy, Falvey and O'Leary;
> Philosophers were there – Thompson and Keller,
> And many a mute and many a talking *fellor*.[41]

Shinkwin was primarily interested in entertainment, and this was made clear by an exhibition he organised in 1828 of 'two Chinese ladies, the only female natives of the Chinese Empire ever seen in Europe,' who apparently possessed diminutive feet and hands that were a wonder to behold.[42] William Thompson and some others attempted to establish an alternative forum where more serious and topical matters could be discussed but the idea was aborted because of differences between the putative organisers.[43]

A much more important event in 1828 than the appearance of two Chinese women in a Cork exhibition hall was the election in July of Daniel

O'Connell as a member of parliament for Clare. O'Connell was the first Catholic candidate to stand in a parliamentary election since the penal laws were enacted. The campaign created feverish excitement throughout the country and in Cork public meetings were organised to demonstrate popular support for O'Connell. On 29 June a meeting of the parishioners of St Peter and Paul's, chaired by Thomas Lyons, was held in the Carey's Lane Catholic chapel. O'Connell's address to the electors of Clare was read and motions were passed praising his candidature and calling for an increase in the 'Catholic rent'.[44] The northside meeting took place the following evening with Jeremiah Murphy of Hyde Park House, Montenotte, presiding. Charles Sugrue made a lengthy speech in support of O'Connell who was a relative of his.[45] Another relative of O'Connell, John O'Connell, also spoke at this meeting. In fact, Cork was somewhat deluged by members of Daniel O'Connell's extended family: other kinsmen involved in the local emancipation movement were William Fagan, Geoffry O'Connell, Herbert Baldwin, and John De Courcey. Another meeting was held on the southside of the city on 1 July with Francis Segarson in the chair.

Sheahan drew up an address on behalf of the people of Cork shortly before polling began in Clare. Following discussions with James J. Hayes and James Lyons (brother of Thomas Lyons) it was decided to embody the address with copies of the resolutions passed at the parish meetings and forward them to Clare by special messenger. At 11p.m. on the night before the polls opened all three went to a printer, John Conner of 14 Tuckey Street, and ordered 2,000 copies of Sheahan's address. These were brought to Clare the following morning by John De Courcey who distributed them at the hustings. Sheahan somewhat flattered himself at a later date when he recounted how O'Connell had allegedly told his friend, Daniel Casey of Dominick Street, that 'whatever hestitation there was in the minds of the Electors about voting for him, was completely removed by the Cork Address'.[46] Nonetheless, as a propagandist with the written word, Sheahan was a useful member of the emancipation movement and the *Chronicle* remained the leading O'Connellite newspaper in Cork. The *Southern Reporter* was tepid in comparison and *The Constitution* was vicious in its attacks on O'Connell and his project.

The Clare election campaign provided an important stimulus for the emancipation movement and O'Connell's victory was an immense achievement. It was clear that he could not actually attend the British parliament but that was of less importance than the confidence that his election inspired throughout Catholic Ireland. 'What is to be done with Ireland?', asked O'Connell after his victory, 'What is to be done with the Catholics? One of two things. They must either crush us or conciliate us'.[47] The Protestant reaction to the election was one of confusion although for ultra-Tories like Gerard Callaghan it represented a clear call to arms. In 1827 the first Brunswick Constitutional Club in Ireland had been formed in Cork as a direct reaction to Catholic moves early in the year to increase the registration of liberal freeholders. The Brunswick Club movement, which soon spread throughout the country, was ultra-Tory in its outlook and its *raison d'être* was to act with the Orangemen as a bulwark against Catholic emancipation. Callaghan was one of its leading figures in Cork and *The Constitution* became an avid supporter of the movement. Indeed, Thomas Townsend, editor of *The Constitution*, served on the committee of the Cork club.[48]

The election of O'Connell gave life to the Cork Brunswick Club. However, it also encouraged increased organisation among the Catholic and Protestant Liberals of the city. Thomas Wyse of Waterford had argued from 1826 for the creation of a permanent electoral machine that could concretely intervene in parliamentary elections in support of Catholic emancipation. The Catholic Association, as it was constituted, was insufficient for this purpose so he formed a Liberal Club in Waterford and promoted the idea of a national organisation. Sheahan admired Wyse, seemingly more than he respected O'Connell, and the *Chronicle* warmly supported the plan for Liberal clubs across the country. In the event, Cork (which already had a cohesive activist core) was one of the first areas to establish such a club.

Daniel O'Connell arrived in Cork in mid-August 1828 and received a tremendous reception. The local emancipationists, operating as the Friends of Civil and Religious Liberty, entertained him at dinner in the large room of the Chamber of Commerce on 14 August. The 253 people present listened to a robust speech in which O'Connell enjoined them to stand up to the 'wretches' of the Friendly Club and force 'bigotry and intolerance [to] give way before the new light of liberty'. He also directed personal invective against Callaghan referring to him as 'a wretch ... presuming on the miseries of his country, and trampling on his father's grave'.[49] Callaghan responded to O'Connell some weeks later when he described him as 'a compound of vanity and vulgar ambition' who had neither 'the mind of a gentleman or the spirit of a true patriot'.[50] On 21 August the Friends of Civil and Religious Liberty hosted a public meeting in the South Parish Catholic chapel at which O'Connell was the main speaker. Charles Beamish, a liberal Protestant, presided and other non-Catholics in attendance included the socialist, William Thompson, who proposed a vote of thanks to O'Connell. Thomas Sheahan was among the speakers at this meeting.[51]

Sheahan published a lengthy pseudonymous letter from himself in the *Chronicle* on the day of the South Parish meeting in which he outlined his ideas for a Liberal club. Fergus O'Ferrall has noted that this letter 'was essentially Wyse's scheme for a national re-organisation of the Catholic movement'.[52] Indeed, it clearly indicates how much in agreement Sheahan was with Wyse on matters of political strategy. He argued for a non-sectarian club that would include all social classes and be willing to fight the Protestant political monopoly even at the local vestry meetings. The Church of Ireland vestry meetings were responsible for the spending of taxes raised in the parish and generally Catholics were allowed to vote only on minor issues. An interesting aspect of Sheahan's letter was his emphasis on the need to properly utilise the print media. He called on the Liberal clubs to use the press 'for the enlightenment of the people' and he especially recommended the use of tracts and catechisms.[53]

Sheahan inserted this letter in the knowledge that O'Connell was in Cork to inaugurate a Liberal club. A 'County and City of Cork Liberal Club' was formed at a meeting chaired by William Thompson in the Chamber of Commerce rooms on 22 August 1828. O'Connell explained the aims of the club which were similar to those of already existing clubs in Waterford, Limerick, Louth and Clare. It was to arrange the collection of the 'Catholic rent'; oppose the Protestant monopoly of corporations in the county; speak out against the tithe system and highlight offending vestries. More than 100 joined and a committee was elected with Thompson as chairman, James John Hayes as secretary, Thomas Lyons as treasurer, and forty others as ordinary committee members. The most prominent members of this large committee included Thomas Sheahan, Dan Meagher, Francis Andrew Walsh (better known as 'Frank Walsh'), John Reynolds, Michael Joseph Barry, James Ludlow Stawell, John Pearce, Richard Dowden, Charles Sugrue, James O'Brien, and William Paul Lyons.[54]

In terms of social position, Sheahan was somewhat down the scale when measured against his fellow committee members. Pearce was his employer. Reynolds was a lawyer. Thompson, Lyons, Meagher, Sugrue, and Barry were either wealthy merchants or manufacturers while James Ludlow Stawell of Innishannon was a Protestant landowner. Frank Walsh, a powerful speaker, was solidly middle class and he later served as professor of law at Queen's College, Cork between 1845 and 1851. Dowden was a mineral water manufacturer who lived in the affluent suburb of Sunday's Well. Hayes, who was an apothecary with premises at 71 Grand Parade, also lived in Sunday's Well and James O'Brien had a thriving army accoutrements business at 16 Tuckey Street. Sheahan, nonetheless, was a key figure because of his editorship of the *Cork Mercantile Chronicle*.

At a meeting the following week this unwieldy committee was broken down and sub-committees created to undertake the practical work of the organisation. These four sub-committees were, a Rent and Finance Committee; a Committee of Civil Rights and Grievances; a Committee of Religious Rights; and a Committee of Parochial Organisation.[55] The first committee dealt with the collection of the 'Catholic rent' and was probably the most important insofar as the *Chronicle* admitted in November that this was the 'most pressing concern' of the club.[56] However, the parochial committee, with twenty people, was the largest sub-committee and its members included Sheahan, Thompson, Sugrue, Dowden, James Daly, and John Reynolds. Sheahan later remarked that he attended nightly meetings of the committee in the clubrooms at 21 Tuckey Street. 'I thought I saw in the Liberal Club,' he wrote, 'the germ of democratic power which exhibited itself subsequently with such effect in the Cork Trades Association; and I felt that no personal sacrifice could be too great on my part to foster it'.[57]

He wrote innumerable articles in the *Chronicle* promoting the organisation and eventually fell ill as a result of his exertions for the committee. James Hayes also suffered from ill-health because of overwork and he was replaced as secretary in November by William Thompson and Charles Sugrue.[58] By November the club membership had increased to over 500 and included many activists from the county like Sheahan's former employer, Rickard Deasy.[59] In general terms, the members were almost entirely middle class but, as O'Ferrall has pointed out, the ethos was 'liberal, reformist, constitutional and democratic'.[60] The connection with the Chamber of Commerce was almost explicit and its public rooms were occasionally used for meetings.

The pressure exerted by the emancipation movement, and especially the impact of the mobilisation around the Clare election, convinced the Westminster government that constitutional change was necessary. Fear of social disorder was the primary reason why Catholic emancipation was granted in April 1829 despite a blocking campaign by the British monarch. The bill granting emancipation was moved swiftly through parliament and the previous oaths of allegiance and abjuration were replaced by an oath of allegiance to the Crown and the Protestant succession. In short, Catholics could now enter parliament and could hold all offices of state except those of Regent, lord chancellor of Ireland (or England), and lord lieutenant of Ireland. Outdoor religious ceremonies were still banned and there remained vexatious restrictions on bishops and religious orders but these were generally ignored.

The achievement of Catholic emancipation was a tremendous victory but it was not unconditional. The 'wings' attached to the act meant the dissolution of the Catholic Association (and the Cork Liberal Club) and the disfranchising of the forty-shilling freeholders who had played such an important role in O'Connell's election in Clare. The raising of the franchise property qualification to £10 freehold effectively reduced the Irish county electorate from more than 216,000 to about 37,000.[61] O'Connell was not happy to lose the forty-shilling freeholders but he was not especially worried by this event either. In essence, he felt that emancipation was worth their sacrifice.

In March 1829 Stephen Coppinger, a leading Dublin-based member of the Catholic Association, attempted to gauge the reaction in his native Cork to the 'sacrifice' of the forty-shilling freeholders. He found that the majority of middle class activists were not greatly concerned about these voters who were mostly working class. In a letter to Thomas Wyse, he lamented that the Chamber of Commerce had become an 'aristocracy of wealth' whose members were eager 'for a share of the loaves and fishes of corruption'. He continued:

In the County and City of Cork News Room, late the Liberal Club, I found Sheehan of the *Chronicle* and a few others disposed for the most part to agree in my views but at the same time they considered that with the members of the Chamber of Commerce who form the *elite* of our public meetings, not merely neutral, but *directly opposed* to us, all chance of getting up a meeting was out of the question.[62]

Thomas Sheahan described the abolition of the forty-shilling freeholder vote, and the restrictions on religious orders, as 'very obnoxious measures' and he helped to organise two petitions from Cork opposing these clauses. 'I contended,' he claimed, 'that the elective franchise required rather to be extended than contracted in Ireland, and that if there was to be any new legislation in regard to it, it should be to protect it by ballot'.[63] In fact, it was not until 1872 that voting by secret ballot was introduced.

It is clear that divisions began to emerge among the Cork liberals almost as soon as the emancipation bill was published. However, these differences were partially set aside following the death on 19 June 1829 of Sir Nicholas Conway Colthurst, one of the city's two MPs. Once again Gerard Callaghan, the ardent Brunswicker, offered himself as a candidate thus creating a scramble among the Liberals for one of their own. Charles Beamish, a brewer who had once chaired an emancipation meeting, was approached by a deputation from the Chamber of Commerce. In his book, *Articles of Irish manufacture* (1833), Sheahan recorded this meeting with distaste. Beamish asked the deputation if it was their intention to bribe during the campaign. 'No,' was the reply. 'Well then,' remarked Beamish, 'you will lose the election', and he declined their invitation to stand.[64]

With no candidate of their own the Liberals, on the suggestion of Dr Herbert Baldwin, decided to approach Sir Augustus Warren, a Tory, to induce him to stand against the hated Callaghan. All they asked of Warren, who agreed to go forward, was that he should not bribe to gain votes. Sheahan's disillusionment with the leading city Liberals deepened during this campaign. He later commented:

> The Liberals . . . did not deserve success – they broke faith with the public – they set out with a pledge not to bribe or sanction bribery; they got money from several persons in aid of the legitimate expenses of the contest, and they expended some hundreds in purchasing votes.[65]

They undermined, he argued, the 'very principle of purity of election' which was what was required for liberal candidates to be elected. Sheahan was a strong believer in the democratic process, even in flawed form. Warren, moreover, failed to appear at the hustings and his later comments indicated that he was a most reluctant candidate.[66]

Gerard Callaghan achieved his ambition and was elected as a member of parliament for Cork city in July 1829. It was, claimed Sheahan, 'the bitterest wormwood to the Liberals' and he left the courthouse early rather than hear the sheriff announce Callaghan's victory. He made his way home to Dominick Street through unfrequented laneways overtaking his fellow activist, John Reynolds, 'who, too, was stealing away from the scene of our mortification'. Reynolds, in despair, said to Sheahan: 'Really, when I see such men triumph, and the suffrage as it is, I am strongly tempted to sell what I have and go to America, and leave this country for ever'. The Chamber of Commerce was the site of much personal altercation later that evening.[67] However, shortly after Callaghan's election it was discovered that he was a government contractor – a circumstance that could lead to his disqualification. Thomas Sheahan, Dan Meagher, and some others, joined forces in an attempt to unseat their enemy and a petition was lodged against him. Because of a prorogation of parliament it was some time before Callaghan's position was decided and the interval was used by Sheahan to raise money to defray the expenses of the petition.

During this time there was much acrimony between political rivals in Cork and Sheahan published attack after attack on Callaghan in the *Chronicle*. He also contributed a sketch to a new Cork-based journal, the *Irish Catholic Magazine*, in which he criticised the leading liberal, Jeremiah Murphy, for not signing the petition against Callaghan and he suggested that it was time for James Daly to atone for his support for Callaghan in the early 1820s.[68] Both Murphy and Daly, like Callaghan, were distillers. Indeed, Sheahan later remarked that Gerard Callaghan was 'the favourite of the great distillers' in 1829 and also had the significant backing of both the National and the Provincial banks.[69] Callaghan reacted against Sheahan's attacks by sending his solicitor to visit John Pearce, proprietor of the *Chronicle*, to threaten a libel action because of a piece published on 20 July. Pearce went to see Callaghan who agreed to forego a prosecution if a paragraph was inserted in the *Chronicle* apologising and pledging that his name would never be alluded to again in the newspaper, either directly or indirectly, in derogatory terms. Consequently, Pearce asked Sheahan to publish the paragraph but he refused and threatened to resign if it was inserted. Eventually, the contentious paragraph was submitted to Daniel O'Connell whose legal and political advice was that it should not be published as 'no honest man will read the *Chronicle*' if it was.[70] John Pearce accepted this assessment and Sheahan retained his position as editor.

Thomas Sheahan and his friends were elated in early 1830 when Callaghan's election was declared invalid and he was barred from contesting the subsequent by-election. Dan Meagher had travelled to London for the conclusion of the case and on 3 March he wrote to Sheahan with the good news:

My dear Sheahan,

I'm sure you'll not attribute my not addressing you before to any want of esteem and respect for you. I now give you the Glorious News, the reward of all our labours. When the Chairman pronounced that 'Gerard Callaghan, Esq. was NOT DULY ELECTED,' my heart leaped from its place, and is now so full, I can write no more than to say, God bless you. Your truly,

Dan Meagher.[71]

The unseating of Gerard Callaghan was a significant morale boost for the Cork Liberals and, allied to the achievement of Catholic emancipation, they had reason to feel satisfied as they entered the 1830s. Sheahan was not quite so sanguine about events. Emancipation, in his opinion, had been achieved at a substantial cost and the by-election of 1829 had shown that the Liberals could bribe with as much alacrity as any Tory. This sense of disillusion ultimately led him away from the Chamber of Commerce and into an engagement with the Cork working class.

The trades, cholera, and the elections in 1832

While the Catholic middle class campaigned for Catholic emancipation, life in working-class Cork remained as bleak as ever. The arrival of emancipation in 1829 had no immediate beneficial impact on the socio-economic difficulties that confronted ordinary workers and their families. Workers in Cork were repeatedly hammered in the years after the end of the Napoleonic wars in 1815. They suffered particularly during the economic crisis of 1816–19; during the crisis of 1822; again in 1826; and in 1832 and early 1833 when the European cholera epidemic finally arrived in Cork city.

In economic terms Cork had prospered in the late-eighteenth century and its provisions trade, in particular, benefited greatly from the American and Napoleonic wars. Until 1782 Cork harbour was the port selected by the British navy and army as the sole provisioner for their supply ships and, in addition, Cork merchants developed important trade links with continental markets like Portugal. Even after the navy rescinded the Cork provisions monopoly the city still supplied nearly two-thirds of wet provisions. Moreover, the continued development of alternative trading markets during the late-eighteenth century meant that Cork export merchants were not completely dependent on government contracts. In 1794, for instance, Cork exported 80 per cent of Irish beef destined for the American continent; in 1795 over 91 per cent of Irish butter dispatched to the same market came through Cork; and in 1799 almost 100 per cent of Irish pork sent to America was shipped from Cork.[1]

However, while not entirely dependent on government contracts, Cork city provisions merchants and their workers suffered considerably from the end of the Napoleonic wars in 1815. The consequent drop in trade at this time was one of a number of factors that assisted a decline in important sectors of the local economy during the 1820s and 1830s. Weavers and coopers were especially hit hard by the crisis of 1816–19. An important element in the decline of the weaving trades was the economic depression that seriously affected Cork's agricultural hinterland after 1818. A consequent drop in disposable income led to a fall in demand for textiles. This depression was impelled by significantly reduced prices in Britain for Irish agricultural produce. In fact, prices began to tumble immediately after the battle of Waterloo though it took some time for these changes to impact on workers.[2] Declining prices should have led to an increase in real wages but this process was interfered with by a collateral rise in unemployment and underemployment.

Interestingly, in a more general sense, Mokyr and Ó Gráda have postulated an apparent rise in average incomes in the half-century before the Famine co-existing with a deterioration in the socio-economic circumstances of the Irish poor.[3] In crude terms, the gap between the poor and the wealthy in Irish society widened.

The economic crisis of 1816–19 affected industry especially because of the reduced demand for textiles.[4] Likewise, the economic downturn of 1826 was damaging for the local textile industry, particularly the linen and cotton sectors, and led to a shrinking of that manufacturing sector in the Cork region. In fact, the contraction of this industry was not entirely related to a reduction in local consumer demand. The final removal of all union duties in 1824 certainly had an impact and the development of machine spinning by water-power (and the consequent establishment of large mills in Britain) led to problems for linen hand-spinners in southern Ireland.[5]

Weaving did not become mechanised as early as spinning but when it did the effect was devastating for the hand-weavers. Edward Donegan, a forty-six year old Cork handloom linen weaver, outlined the devastation that his branch of the weaving trade had suffered when he gave evidence before the Irish poor inquiry of 1834. Emigration to England by handloom workers had begun in earnest in 1810 and Donegan estimated that 4,000 to 5,000 families had left the city and its environs since then. Manchester was a favourite destination and once there the weavers continued to work on handlooms but were able to add to their incomes by sending their children to work in the factories.[6] The figure given by Donegan seems remarkably high but Thomas Sheahan similarly indicated that at the end of the eighteenth century in the city of Cork and its immediate vicinity 20,000 individuals and their families subsisted on the various branches of weaving.[7] In fact, Henry Sadlier, whose substantial linen and cotton business was based at Lawton's Quay and in Glasheen, claimed in 1795 that 10,000 people were employed by his company alone.[8] The once-numerous weavers of Cork, like those in the rest of southern Ireland, either emigrated, joined the ranks of the labourers, or continued to eke out an increasingly precarious existence from their trade.

The failure of the Cork linen and cotton industries to successfully mechanise, allied to the growth of steam navigation, meant that competition from the large English and Irish mills ultimately undermined the local trade. Dark clouds continued to gather above the handloom weavers but in fact their day had begun to dusk as soon as the new machinery appeared. It is difficult to quantify the social impact of the weavers demise in a small city like Cork but it must have been considerable if only because of the sheer numbers that the trade and its ancillaries once employed. It was a doomed trade though the weavers retained some strength until at least the mid-1820s and did not completely disappear until the 1890s.[9] By 1834 Sheahan counted as few as 400 journeymen weavers in the Cork city area – 200 cotton weavers, eighty tape and stocking weavers, sixty woollen weavers, and sixty worsted weavers.[10] Edward Donegan made it clear that wages had dropped and their living was often precarious. In 1831 he was able to earn 1s. per day which was a substantial reduction of the 2s. per day that he had earned in earlier years. By 1834 he found, however, that he was earning just 6d. or 8d. for a day's work. Lodgings for his 'class', he explained, consisted of two families sharing a single room at a rent of 6d. to 9d. a week and he frequently had to work all day on one meal of potatoes.[11] This was a labourer's existence and Donegan clearly felt these changes as a diminishment of what he had grown to expect as his standard of living.

Another trade that was under increasing pressure was that of coopering. The coopers had prospered while the export salt-provisions trade boomed but the ending of the war with France led to serious unemployment and the coopers never really regained their former status. The available figures regarding the numbers employed in coopering in the fifty years before 1832 are not exact but they do indicate a general downward trend.[12]

Table 2. Coopers working in Cork city, 1782–1832

	Journeymen	Apprentices	Working masters
1782	1,500	300	n.a.
1799	1,200	n.a.	n.a.
1815	800	n.a.	n.a.
1828	700	180	100
1832	485	183	93

Source: *Cork Mercantile Chronicle* 27 January 1832; Thomas Sheahan, *Irish destitution in 1834* (Cork, 1834) pp 17–18; 23.

The decline in the provisions trade as a result of the peace badly affected the coopers but they were also hit by the extended export of livestock as a result of the emergence of steam navigation. In addition, the equalisation of the salt duty in England and Ireland increased the virulence of English competition further damaging the local trade.[13] Of the 485 journeymen coopers counted by Sheahan in early 1832, fourteen were in the House of Industry and Mendicity Asylum while roughly thirty were in constant employment in the local breweries and distilleries. The remaining 440 or so coopers were living in straitened circumstances – sixty-eight (with family members amounting to 213 individuals) had not got a single day's work during 1831 while the others had found only partial employment. The butter market provided consistent work for a section of the trade but it was not full-year employment and the months between November and March were moribund.[14] The penury that followed from less employment was clear in the coopers' diet which in the early 1830s consisted of potatoes and milk twice a day sometimes varied with herrings. On Sundays meat was often eaten but not every Sunday.[15] Sheahan also remarked that these partially employed coopers were 'wretchedly circumstanced with regard to bedding; furniture they have scarcely any; [and] the pawn offices are bursting with their little articles of clothing'.[16] This was a picture of immiseration and the coopers fortunes continued to decline through the remainder of the nineteenth century.

It would be wrong to say that all tradesmen suffered like the weavers and the coopers. Some trades rarely, or only occasionally, felt the pressures of severe unemployment or persistent underemployment while others like the chandlers, hatters, and the cutlers believed that they had been run close to extinction by English competition and the Act of Union itself.[17] It is clear that at the beginning of the 1830s working class Cork considered itself on the edge of economic destitution. The plight of the coopers, in particular, was strongly felt by Thomas Sheahan and in early 1832 he highlighted their miserable circumstances in the *Cork Mercantile Chronicle*.[18] Sheahan's house at 25 Dominick Street was situated in an area long associated with the coopers and where many lived in the vicinity of the butter exchange and the distilleries in nearby Blackpool. In addition, he referred enigmatically at one stage to a previous unprofitable experience of his own with the trade and it may be that he had some familial links with the coopers.[19] This is possible as his father, who seems to have died *circa* 1830, was a carpenter as well as being a funeral undertaker.

In general the poor circumstances of many in working-class Cork only became a matter for serious public discourse during periods of obvious crisis. The reasons for this are plain and have much to do with the contemporary state policy of minimal intervention in matters of social welfare. Landowners, merchants and manufacturers might make voluntary donations towards health and mendicity facilities but the state imposed no obligations on them to pay taxes to support any form of legal provision for the poor. The idea of Irish poor laws had been a source of argument in the parlours of middle-class Cork since at least 1826 and for the many who opposed such legal provisions the predicament of the destitute was best ignored.

In the event, Cork workers did not have to wait inordinately long after 1826 before another crisis accentuated their miserable conditions. A cholera epidemic confronted Europe in 1831 for the first time. Cholera had long been endemic in India but the rapid growth of trade as the British empire expanded meant that by the early nineteenth century the deadly disease had spread to the borders of the European continent. In late 1830 it reached Moscow from where it was exported to Poland in 1831 with Russian troops sent to suppress a rebellion in that country.[20] This westward progression continued and by 5 October 1831 cholera had signalled its arrival in the important German port of Hamburg. A few weeks later the disease claimed its first victims in England.[21] It was clear that Ireland would eventually fall to its onward march.

Cholera was a new disease for Europeans and an especially frightening one. First of all, it was a virulent disease that affected every class in society with symptoms that were truly terrifying and demeaning. Its arrival was unpredictable and its effects often of some demographic importance. Reporting on its incidence in Berlin in October 1831 the *Southern Reporter* shuddered that it continued 'to thin the population' of that city.[22] In fact, there were 1,423 deaths in Berlin in 1831 from 2,274 cases of cholera or a death rate of 6.2 per 1,000 of the population.[23] Cholera moved with alarming speed and seemed to contemporaries to bear more of the resonance of plague than disease. Little was known about its causes and treatments were purely experimental. Popular fear led to widespread riots in both the Russian and Habsburg Empires as elements of the peasantry reacted violently against what they believed was a government plot to wipe them out.[24] A more mundane reaction, and one which was ultimately shared by the people of Cork, was non-attendance at the funerals of victims and a shunning of their immediate family. The symptoms of cholera were appalling and bound to inspire such terror and incomprehension. Within a matter of hours a victim was transformed into a sunken-eyed, blue-skinned physical wreck. There was a huge loss of bodily fluids, constant vomiting, and the defecation of massive amounts of diarrhoea. It was a distressing, violent, and demeaning exit from the world.

Quarantine regulations were revised in late 1831 and ships arriving in Cork harbour from Russian and Baltic ports were required to go to Milford for quarantine procedures. However, pressure from local merchants ensured that most vessels could actually quarantine in Cork itself although by December ships from ports within the affected parts of Europe were obliged to produce certificates to prove that they were free of cholera and all bedding and clothing was inspected by local officials.[25] It is unclear what the officials expected to find in the bedding or clothing (probably fleas) but the exercise was important as psychological consolation to a worried populace.

If the populace was worried it was not panic-stricken. This was evident from the meagre attendance at a public meeting convened by the mayor of Cork, John Besnard, at the city courthouse on 16 November to discuss the possibility of a local outbreak.[26] Besnard had first arranged a meeting on 9 November with the Protestant and Catholic clergy of the city where he informed them that under legislation vestries in parishes with 1,000 or more members could create 'officers of health' within a month of 25 March each year. As March had passed he indicated that he and his fellow magistrates were willing to facilitate the immediate appointment of such officials.[27] Cholera was now prevalent in Sunderland in England and, understandably, it was believed that its arrival in Ireland was imminent.[28] On 15 November vestry meetings were held and five officers of health were appointed for each of the seven city parishes. The public meeting convened by the mayor on the following day was intended to discuss these developments and to suggest a strategy for further action.

The attendance at the meeting was small but it did include both Tories and Liberals and in that sense indicated that a united approach was possible. It seems that there were fewer Liberals present than Tories with Dan Meagher, Francis B. Beamish, William Crawford, and Thomas Sheahan the only prominent members of that faction who spoke. John Boyle, the proprietor and editor of *The Freeholder*, was also present but he was of little real importance in Liberal circles except as a humorist. Sheahan, who was among the officers of health appointed in St Mary's parish, intimated that he expected to be put in a position where he could provide blankets, straw, and food for the estimated 4,000 destitute in his parish. Money was a key concern and much of the discussion turned on how the new officials and any anti-cholera campaign were to be paid for. A voluntary fund had been established by the mayor but it was also suggested that monies be raised through local taxes. Gerard Callaghan and Dan Meagher formed an uncommon alliance in opposing the levying of a tax but the meeting eventually agreed that this should be done when the time became appropriate. One of the most important decisions taken by the meeting was the formation of a Central Committee of Health to solicit and dispense funds subject to representations from the legally appointed officers of health.[29] The Committee of Health, however, had no statutory basis and represented little more than the goodwill of its members. Sheahan was later to criticise its alleged lassitude and practical ineffectiveness.

At a meeting of the corporation on 17 November the officers of health were formally accepted and it was decided to adopt the public meeting recommendation that a tax be levied if or when the parish vestries deemed it necessary.[30] The weight given to the opinion of the vestries meant that the proposed taxes could be presented as voluntary assessments. It seemed as if serious efforts were being made to prepare for the coming epidemic. However, by January 1832 it was clear that the corporation and the Committee of Health had failed to provide the necessary infrastructure to deal with a cholera outbreak. Meetings of the Committee of Health were well attended but not, claimed the *Chronicle*, 'to the extent which might have been reasonably expected'.[31] Sites had still not been decided on for emergency hospitals and the issue of poor laws began to dominate discussion.

At a meeting of the Committee of Health on 16 January a motion was passed calling on John Besnard, the mayor, to summon a public meeting for the purpose of drawing up a petition to Westminster demanding a system of poor laws in Ireland. Besnard, who was opposed to poor laws, initially attempted to stall proceedings by requesting that he first be presented with a formal requisition signed by proponents of the meeting.[32] However, eventually it became clear that he had no intention of summoning any public meeting. In fact, Besnard bluntly explained that he had an 'antipathy' to public meetings and was opposed to them in general.[33] Acrimonious disputes occurred over the issue at committee meetings held on 23 and 30 January with Francis B.

Beamish, William Crawford, Michael J. Barry and Thomas Sheahan among the Liberals who argued strongly for a public meeting. Ranged against them were the Tories and many leading local O'Connellites who were aware of Daniel O'Connell's aversion to Irish poor laws. Barry succinctly identified their opposition:

> There were two parties opposed to Poor Laws in Cork – the one, what he would call . . . the Ascendancy party. These did not think it just that their properties should be taxed to support those who had none . . . The others were those who imagined that, in the present circumstances, any difference of opinion with Mr. O'Connell's declared sentiments on the subject, would endanger the interests of the country, by inducing the Government to believe that his popularity was not so firm or so extended as every Irishman would wish to impress on them.[34]

The dispute on this issue continued through February and became a serious source of friction among those who were supposed to be preparing for the approaching epidemic.[35] Moreover, it is clear that Barry was correct in highlighting divisions within the Liberal camp. These were manifested at a meeting in the city courthouse on 9 February when a vote to hold the public meeting was narrowly passed by sixteen to twelve. Among those opposed to convening a poor law meeting were Dr Herbert Baldwin and James J. Hayes and, importantly, many leading O'Connellites did not even bother to attend this preliminary gathering. In the event, a committee to organise the meeting was established and it included some prominent figures like Richard Dowden, Thomas Sheahan, James Daly and William Fagan.[36] The inclusion of Fagan, a relative of O'Connell, was an especially important indicator of the confused conflict within local Liberalism as he would normally have aligned himself with Meagher and the moderate element in the Chamber of Commerce. Baldwin, on the other hand, would normally have been expected to take the radical side of the argument and to stand with Sheahan and Dowden.

While the poor law debate heated up the officers of health who had been appointed in late 1831 carried out a census of the poor in urban Cork (table 3).[37] The results proved shocking to those who spent little time in working class districts.

Those registered as 'distressed' in this survey were living from hand to mouth, surviving on casual employment, and not in a position to support themselves during a period of sickness. The individuals listed as 'destitute' were those who survived largely by begging, by collecting manure for sale, and by other precarious means. Those in this category were invariably denuded of clothes, except for rags worn during the day, and they slept on straw at night without any covering. In a city of 86,534 inhabitants, a figure of 23,021

Table 3. Census of poor in Cork city in early 1832

Parishes	Population	'Distressed poor'	'Destitute'
St Anne's	18,475	5,189	1,000
St Nicholas	17,642	5,602	2,000
St Finbarr's	14,522	3,274	1,000
St Mary's	13,357	5,311	1,000
Holy Trinity	9,567	1,251	400
St Peter's	7,943	1,932	600
St Paul's	5,028	462	250

Source: Figures taken from *First report of the royal commission into the condition of the poorer classes in Ireland. Appendix C – Part I*, H.C. 1836 [35], xxx, p. 24.

'distressed', and 6,250 'destitute', was clearly bad news. In such circumstances, any addition to the economic problems of the working class (whether from an economic downturn or the expense of sickness in terms of lost income) was inevitably going to have a devastating impact.

During January 1832 Sheahan became increasingly exasperated with the apparent indifference of many of the more affluent citizens of Cork to the possible consequences of a cholera outbreak. Attempts were made to secure the use of military hospitals but Dublin Castle and the military authorities denied these requests.[38] Sheahan and his friend, Daniel Casey, were officers of health for the Shandon parish of St Mary's and they were acutely aware of the precarious nature of life for large numbers in that district. He supported the recently revived demand for the repeal of the Act of Union but he argued that the poor 'if left to perish on, whilst we are experimenting, may, without securing permanent good to themselves, entail much wretchedness upon others'.[39] In other words, a failure to deal with poverty could result in understandable social turmoil. At a meeting of the Committee of Health in late January he challenged the inaction:

> Now, Gentlemen, you are not prepared by voluntary contributions to give even blankets to the poor. There does not appear to me to be a very anxious desire to go to the Lord Lieutenant lest the Citizens should have to repay a loan by an inequitable assessment. What then will you do?[40]

He continued his attack in the *Cork Mercantile Chronicle* where he demanded that something tangible be done. In an editorial Sheahan criticised his former friends in the Chamber of Commerce for their lack of civic responsibility:

We have asked already, and we ask again, why do not the practical patriots of the Chamber of Commerce, who do not pretend to be either Nobility or Gentry, why do they not concert measures for bringing before the Legislature the complaints of every Parish in this City and County against the system which they in common with us reprobate. We at least have done *our* duty.[41]

In another column he published a series of mock reports of a cholera epidemic in Cork in which he accentuated the impact such an event would have on the city. At the foot of this column he printed the following notice:

A REWARD!!!

A handsome reward will be given to any persons who shall invent a MACHINE *by which the Poor may be supported without troubling the Rich.* Applications for further information to be made at the houses of those who have not yet contributed to the Cholera fund, or at the houses of those who have contributed one Pound for every twenty they ought.[42]

Sheahan's anger was palpable and it increased as he moved among the poor in his own locality examining their miserable housing conditions.[43] He also championed the cause of the journeymen coopers who were in a wretched state and demanding government-assisted emigration schemes. In a letter to Sheahan the coopers expressed their 'heartfelt gratitude' for his support and they explained that their committee had found members of the trade 'in a perfect state of nudity, excepting that they had an appearance of a petticoat'.[44] Often, this resulted from the pawning of good clothes and an inability to redeem them.

These events occurred against a background of heightened political activity. Most liberals and O'Connellites, including Sheahan, supported the intensified campaign against the payment of tithes in the early 1830s. The 'tithe war' of 1830–33 was invigorated by raised Catholic expectations following emancipation and by an agricultural depression that increased hostility to the religious levies. O'Connell did not directly involve himself in the campaign, partly because of some associated violence. Fourteen people, for instance, were killed by yeomanry during an affray at Newtownbarry in County Wexford on 18 June 1831 while a process-server and twelve policemen were attacked and killed at Carrickshock in County Kilkenny on 14 December that year. In general, however, the campaign was one of passive resistance and the *Cork Mercantile Chronicle* was particularly supportive.

In addition to the tithe war, the Act of Union became a serious political issue from 1830 onwards as O'Connell and his allies demanded its repeal. Commitment to 'repeal' was required from candidates in the general election of late 1832 before O'Connell would grant his endorsement. As early as October 1830 Sheahan had helped to organize a 1,000 strong banquet in favour of repeal. His fellow-organizers included Edward Lane, Morgan O'Donovan, and John Creedon, all of whom would later be prominent in the Cork Trades Association. The Chamber of Commerce declined to associate itself with this demonstration which was almost entirely working class in composition.[45] As well as the campaign against the tithes and for repeal, Irish Liberals also strongly urged support for a reform of the parliamentary franchise that was then being discussed in London. In fact, a large rally in support of 'reform' was held in Cork at Nelson Place (since renamed Emmet Place) on 17 October 1831 with 16,000 people present. Sheahan had been among the requisitionists who called this meeting although he did not play a prominent part in the actual event.[46]

The continued popularity of Daniel O'Connell, and working-class support for repeal, was clearly demonstrated on 18 March 1832 when he made a triumphal entry into Cork city. This stage-managed 'public entry' was organised by a committee of fifteen elected at a meeting, chaired by Thomas Lyons, in the Chamber of Commerce rooms. An important innovation was the involvement of the city tradesmen. Indeed, tradesmen, who had their own sections in the procession, dominated the demonstration and this appears to have been their first direct organised intervention in political life in Cork. Moreover, the huge march from Riverstown into Patrick Street attracted probably the largest numbers ever seen at a public demonstration in the city. The *Chronicle* estimated the crowd as numbering tens of thousands.[47] The O'Connell procession undoubtedly infused confidence in the politically-minded tradesmen of the city and was probably a significant step on the road to the formation of the Cork Trades Association in June that year.

This demonstration allows us some insight into the level of organisation among the trades in Cork in 1832. It is clear that an enormous amount of effort was expended in the weeks before the event and each trade that participated arrived with elaborate banners, flags, and other paraphernalia. The *Chronicle* named twenty-seven trades that took part: the house-painters, bakers, chandlers, glovers, sawyers, tailors, tobacco-makers, paper-makers, brogue-makers, harness and collar-makers, stone-cutters, wheelwrights, smiths, victuallers, curriers, cotton and worsted-weavers, masons, glass cutters and makers, cabinet-makers, slaters and plasterers, nailors, hatters, coachmakers, wool-combers, brush and bellow-makers, carpenters, and printers. In addition, there was a section for unattached tradesmen and one for salters (who were effectively semi-skilled labourers).[48] Each of these groups marched behind their 'mortality societies' or their trade unions. The unions (commonly known as 'combinations') had been decriminalised in 1824 but many still operated in a hazy netherworld, often preferring to pass themselves off as simply mortality societies which existed to take care of their members families in times of need. Two peculiar omissions from the list of participants are the shoemakers and the coopers as both these trades had a long history of organisation.

An analysis of the slogans and mottoes inscribed on the trades' banners at the demonstration is of some interest. The *Chronicle* identifies eighty-three inscriptions. Only two refer to societies – the 'Society of Painters' and the 'Cork Victuallers' – while eighteen refer directly to O'Connell. In terms of the political issues of the day, there were no references to tithes, one to the need for poor laws (the sawyers), nine to reform, and twenty to repeal. The weavers were particularly pointed in their attitude to the repeal issue, declaring: 'We are the victims of the Union'. O'Connell's name was commonly coupled with the demand for repeal while William IV, the British monarch, was coupled with the slogan of 'reform'. It is obvious from the many images of both O'Connell and the king that Cork tradesmen were at pains to stress the constitutional parameters of their aspirations. They were not seeking a republic or, at least, such views were not overtly displayed. There were, not surprisingly, no references to 1798 or to the United Irishmen and only two to Grattan's parliament. Trade union slogans were few although on one banner the hatters inscribed, 'We assist each other in time of need', and the smiths used the motto, 'By hammer and hand all arts do stand'.[49]

Cholera eventually arrived in Cork a few weeks after the O'Connell demonstration. On 5 April the first case appeared when an eleven-year-old girl fell ill at 8 a.m. and died later that night. The disease did not show itself again to any great extent until eight days later when several cases occurred in the neighbourhood of the Coal Quay and Paul Street.[50] Thereafter it spread quickly through the city. By this stage Thomas Sheahan and Daniel Casey had become entirely disillusioned with their positions as officers of health and they resigned on 23 April. At a St Mary's vestry meeting Sheahan argued that an 'assessment' (or tax) of 1s. in the pound should be levied instead of the proposed 4d. in order to deal with the increased destitution. This was rejected. Sheahan further asserted that he had not met any member of the Committee of Health 'in the abodes of wretchedness with which the Parish abounded' or 'going with the cholera bier to the threshold of the pauper' to enquire 'what predisposed him for disease, and what comforts he would have at home when returning convalescent from the hospital'. He also announced at this meeting that he had not paid minister's money, or church rates, for the previous year and he would never pay them again.[51]

By 27 April Cork had suffered 606 cases of cholera including 174 deaths.[52] Sheahan blamed the wealthy in Cork society for these deaths: 'they were hungry, and the men of wealth fed them not – they were naked, and they clad them not – they were cold and they warmed them not'. He argued that the wealthy had failed in their 'obligations to humanity'.[53] In fact, Sheahan believed that the death-rate from cholera would have been much lower were it not for poverty, filth, and congestion in the working-class districts. Ultimately, between April 1832 and early 1833 there were 4,945 cholera cases in the city that resulted in 1,619 deaths or 18.8 per 1,000 of the population.[54] This was a significant death-rate and exceeded that suffered in cities like Berlin which in 1832 had 1.8 deaths per 1,000 of the population.[55]

Emergency hospitals were established in various parts of the city and a Board of Health, with legal powers, was sanctioned by the government at the end of April.[56] To fund the medical services monies were raised through voluntary donations and by a local tax or 'voluntary assessment'. In addition, the government eventually loaned £10,000 to the Board of Health – in April 1834 the local authorities were still refusing to pay back this money.[57] Meanwhile, Sheahan and Casey made their own effort to deal with poverty and hunger in the Dominick Street area. An anonymous donor supplied them with funds and they set up a soup kitchen and distributed blankets to the poor. In the *Chronicle* Sheahan described food and fuel as 'the best anti-cholerics'.[58] He also called on the officers of health to protest about the meagre funds that they were allocated:

> What is to be done to protect the lives of all, and to save our City from being even still more over-run by widows and orphans? Officers of Health! In the name of our fellow-citizens, we call upon you to do your duty. You have not funds to execute your functions. The miserable sums which the Central Committee has voted to you, are of no service than to bring out the destitution of your respective parishes – you see it – but you cannot relieve it. Apply then forthwith to the Government for 'food, fuel, and raiment' for the poor of your respective parishes – consider not by whom that money is to be repaid – to save life is your first duty – discharge it – or give back your trust.[59]

By early June, Sheahan and his friends realised that their own efforts to relieve the poor were insufficient. He later explained that they were 'not able to give one substantial meal in the day to one-tenth of the poor of the parish' and their funds were soon exhausted.[60] A meeting was held where it was decided that the problem of poverty could not be resolved through alms and, consequently, Sheahan pushed for the establishment of a movement to promote Irish manufactures as a means of reviving local industry.

On 8 June the *Cork Mercantile Chronicle* published an advertisement signed by fifty-seven householders calling on the inhabitants of St Mary's parish to attend a public meeting three days later 'to concert measures for the encouragement of Irish manufactures'. The names on this list are interesting insofar as they mostly represented a particular stratum in Cork society. These were Thomas Sheahan's people – the *petite bourgeoisie* of his locality – shopkeepers, publicans and small businessmen. With the exception of Sheahan, and possibly Arthur O'Leary, none of those who called the meeting were prominent in local Liberal or O'Connellite politics. James Daly, a self-made distiller who was on friendly terms with Sheahan, was recruited to preside at the meeting which was held in Dominick Street in the premises of Messrs. Thompson and McCarthy. Daly, who was originally from Carrigtwohill, had lived in the parish for forty years and he was the only individual with substantial wealth at the meeting.[61] The most prominent contributors to the discussion (apart from Sheahan) included a vintner, a skin buyer, a grocer/tobacconist, a chandler/shopkeeper, a chandler/vintner, a butter merchant, two grocers, a weaver, and a linen draper.[62] All of these lived within the immediate vicinity of Dominick Street with the exception of Edward Donegan, the weavers' leader, who made a stirring speech outlining the woes of his trade.

An Irish Manufacture Association was formed in St Mary's parish and membership was soon close to 100.[63] Sheahan, who was widely accepted as the founder, encouraged the formation of branches in other city parishes. In the event, the movement proved an immediate success with four active associations formed covering all the city parishes with the exception of Holy Trinity.[64] Moreover, an Irish manufacture association was established in Dublin on 29 June and this organisation was in close contact with the Cork movement.[65] Sheahan was credited at the Irish poor inquiry of 1834 with having begun this resurgence of interest in Irish industry.[66] Ultimately, however, despite winning the support of local merchants and manufacturers, the success of the Cork movement was ephemeral and it had contracted by November 1832 when the remnants of the parish branches united into one centralised organisation.[67]

The most durable, and arguably the most important, initiative of the Irish manufactures movement was the creation on the 25 June of the Cork Trades Association. For Sheahan the movement begun on 11 June was primarily intended as a method of increasing employment for the tradesmen of Cork city. The promotion of Irish products involved a natural convergence with the interests of local manufacturers but while their involvement was encouraged so too was that of local tradesmen. The unionist *Constitution* was alert to the possible implications of the new movement at an early stage. Within a few days of the emergence of the Irish Manufacture Association it commended efforts to find work for the unemployed tradesman but warned that 'it is not seemly that others should labour to turn him into a party tool, to be employed for ends that will ever be contested while attempted by a party'.[68] In fact, Sheahan had already set about persuading the tradesmen to establish their own organisation and a mass demonstration on 25 June was used as the platform from which to launch this new group.

More than 30,000 people gathered at Warren's Place and on the South Mall for this second trades demonstration of 1832.[69] It was an immense show of strength in favour of local manufactures but it was also an indication of the growing political confidence of local tradesmen. At 12.30 a.m. the procession left from Coppinger's Corner, at the northern end of Warren's Place, and made its way along Merchants Quay. At the head of the march was a large banner on which was painted a female representation of Ireland standing beside a harp. On the right of this figure was a gaunt-looking tradesman, ragged and famished, to whom the representative female was holding out the hand of relief. On her left, above her, was the Genius of Plenty pouring out from his cornucopia the abundance of the land, wheat, honey, fruit, and other agricultural produce. 'The Revival of Irish Manufacture' was inscribed on this banner. Thirty-nine trades participated in the procession, along with three or four bands, and the crowd was huge by the time it reached Patrick's bridge. Interestingly, each trade halted opposite the Chamber of Commerce on Patrick Street where they either cheered or had their bands play national airs.[70] This gesture was a clear indication of the accepted importance of that institution in the civic life of the city.

The demonstration made its way through the city centre, across Parliament bridge and up Sullivan's Quay, before moving down the old Main Street to the North-Gate bridge where it was met by a large group representing the northside branches of the Irish Manufacture Association. William Ring of Mallow Lane, an officer of health in the Shandon parish of St Anne's and a leading association member, stepped forward and read an address on behalf of the 'northerners' welcoming the procession into their side of the city. A tour of the northern districts followed before the marchers eventually rallied at Sydney Place to listen to speeches that were mostly made by tradesmen. The orators, most of whom became leading figures in the trades association, included Cornelius Carver, a bookbinder of 4 Paul Street; Edward Donegan, the weaver; Morgan F. O'Donovan, an engraver and copper-plate printer of 10 Carey's Lane; and John Creedon.[71] Both Carver and Donegan had attended the first meeting of the Irish Manufacture Association in Dominick Street.[72]

Following the rally a committee was established which met for two nights at the Carey's Lane schoolrooms before it was decided to form the Cork Trades Association.[73] Edward Lane, a tailor of 1 Grattan Street, became the chairman of this new organisation while Morgan O'Donovan and John Creedon became joint-secretaries. The treasurer was Andrew Roche of Sullivan's Quay, a middle-class man of independent means. It seems that Roche was selected for this position because it was felt that he was 'more fitted' to it than 'a mechanic'. Financial practicalities may have determined the choice of treasurer but from the outset, while always remaining the dominant element, the tradesmen desired to win the favour of affluent liberals. Radical Liberals and non-tradesmen like Thomas Sheahan, Andrew Roche, Frank Walsh, and Francis B. Beamish regularly attended the meetings and exerted considerable influence. Sheahan was undoubtedly the most important figure in this group and he virtually turned the *Chronicle* into an organ of the trades association. Others like the Unitarians, Richard Dowden and Isaac Varian, made infrequent appearances while the wealthier element at the Chamber of Commerce (Lyons, Sugrue, Meagher, Fagan, and so on) steered clear of the new organisation until electoral exigencies compelled a collaboration.

In its initial stages the Cork Trades Association clearly saw itself as a branch of the Irish manufactures movement that, in turn, was a response to the continuing cholera epidemic. However, simmering resentments soon came to the surface. For example, at the trades demonstration on 25 June one speaker, a hairdresser named Dorney, had complained: 'Your Aristocrats will have no man cut his hair who has not a Cockney accent (*hear, and cheers*). I know myself an instance where a man from England got 6s. a week more than an Irishman . . . and this merely because he had an English accent (*hear, and laughter*)'.[74] Those who spoke at this rally were aware that their problems were exacerbated rather than caused by the cholera outbreak. Edward Donegan claimed that they were 'victims of misrule and British monopoly' and he blamed the Act of Union for the social misery that Cork was experiencing. He called on women, in particular, to join in their movement:

> The ladies of Ireland should recollect that the women of Carthage cut their golden tresses to make bows for their heroes to defend their country. Is an Irishwoman less sensitive to the feelings of patriotism? Did not the American ladies when Britain endeavoured to tax the only country which ever had a real representative system of Government, did not the women, I say, of Boston break their tea pots, and say that they would never submit to British tyranny?[75]

Donegan also made an appeal to Protestant workers to recognise the negativities of the union with Britain. Born in 1788 he was a republican as well as a vigorous labour activist. His personal circumstances were miserable and his anger was genuine. He and his young family lived in one room, possibly sharing with another family, and as a weaver he endured long periods of unemployment which had reduced him to breaking stones for paltry wages. At a women's public meeting in October, he poignantly expressed his despair at 'the famished appearance' of his wife and 'the hungry cries' of his children.[76]

Donegan was not alone in blaming the Act of Union for the decline of Irish industry and the Cork Trades Association rapidly moved from promoting Irish manufactures to demanding the repeal of the legislative union with Britain. Despite protestations to the contrary the trades association was clearly a working class political organisation. Its antagonism to the unionist establishment in Cork was confirmed in early July when an Irish manufactures meeting planned for Blarney was banned by the mayor, John Besnard. Thomas Sheahan, Cornelius Carver, Morgan O'Donovan, and John Creedon were among a large group that travelled to Blarney on the appointed day to confront their obstructers. They were faced with a large force of soldiers and policemen armed with four six-pounder cannons. Sheahan, as the principal organiser, demanded that the meeting be allowed to proceed but this was rejected by the magistrates.[77] The Cork Trades Association was outraged by this event and when the lord lieutenant visited the city in August, Edward Lane, O'Donovan, and Creedon waited on him on behalf of the association. The banning of the Blarney meeting was forthrightly condemned by Lane and he informed the lord lieutenant that the organisers 'had been treated worse than aliens in the land of their fathers'.[78]

The general election of late 1832 provided the trades association with an opportunity to establish itself as a significant force in local political life. Daniel O'Connell declared his intention to endorse only those candidates who openly espoused pro-repeal sentiments and it was apparent that his objective, which the Cork tradesmen supported, was the creation of a significant Irish repeal lobby in the British parliament. On 13 August Dr Herbert Baldwin of Camden Place, a Catholic medical doctor and landowner, announced his intention to run in the two-seat Cork city constituency as a repealer and as an advocate of reform.[79] In his political outlook Baldwin was a radical liberal and he was supportive of the recent liberal revolutions on the continent, especially that in Poland.[80] Thomas Sheahan almost immediately signalled his support in the *Chronicle* although he did have some private reservations.[81] Baldwin had a fiery temperament and following an election defeat in 1830 both he and Frank Walsh had repeatedly challenged one of the victors, Daniel Callaghan, to a duel because of a perceived slight. Callaghan ultimately had to seek the protection of the law and he brought a suit alleging that he was being induced to act illegally.[82] Sheahan elicited a pledge from Baldwin to refrain from duelling before he agreed to back his candidature.

The Liberals began to prepare for the coming election in August when an eleven-man registry committee (which included Meagher, Sheahan, Beamish, Sugrue, Lyons, Fagan, Daly, and Hayes) was elected at a meeting in the Theatre Royal in George's Street to give life to the 1832 Reform Act by persuading those affected to formally register for the vote.[83] Sheahan was one of those who voted for the first time in 1832.[84] Meagher was the leading figure in this registration campaign – it was later remarked that for three weeks he stood at his post 'defying cholera and chloride of lime, and inhaling the mephitic atmosphere of the Tuckey-street guard-house' while registering voters.[85] On 10 September the *Chronicle* published a detailed synopsis of the provisions of the Reform Act in a further attempt to encourage registration. The Tories, in contrast, attempted to dissuade registration and a placard was posted about the town misinforming 'poor householders' that if they registered for the vote they would entail an annual charge of £4 13s. 4d. on themselves.[86]

The Cork Trades Association maintained an ostensibly neutral position on the election until mid-October. Indeed, when Francis Bernard Beamish, the wealthy brewer, formally became a member of the association in August he expressed his satisfaction that 'political questions' were excluded from discussion.[87] Beamish, however, was being wilfully blind. While repeal was not openly discussed at that time there were many allusions to the issue and it was obvious that the tradesmen supported the O'Connellite position. On 16 October this was clarified when, following a visit to the trades association rooms in Nelson Place by Baldwin and Feargus O'Connor, it was decided to rescind the rule disallowing political discussion. O'Connor, who would later become the leader of Chartism in Britain, was running as a repeal candidate in the county constituency. Donegan and Sheahan both spoke in favour of adopting repeal as the policy of the organisation although Sheahan was adamant that their commitment had to be more than verbal. The issue of widespread voter bribery at previous elections was high on his list of concerns and he asked the members:

> Had they made up their minds to loathe in the shop and in the street, in public and in private, the wretch who would take a bribe, or the reprobate who would tender it. There are thirty or forty electors at Glasheen, weavers, for whom we have done some good – for whom we are determined to do more. I ask Mr. Donegan will he bring them into this room to pledge themselves one and all, in the presence of their country, that they will vote for two Repealers, and that they will vote without money?[88]

Donegan admitted that there were two 'bad' men among these weavers but he promised to bring in the rest.

In an effort to link up with the wider O'Connellite movement, Charles Sugrue was invited to preside at a trades association public meeting on 18 October. He lauded the organisation in an introductory speech: 'From a mere trades union you start into matured existence, one of those political unions which have wrought so much weal for England'. Sheahan rose to propose that a committee be established to assist in the return of two repealers for Cork city. He suggested that this committee should include one delegate from each trade, one from each of the labourers' societies, and twelve from nominations at the meeting. This was a strategy for directly linking the trades societies with the association. Baldwin entered the room as Sheahan was speaking causing him to remark that at least they had one repealer in the city that they could fully endorse. Frank Walsh seconded the proposal for a committee and, interestingly, he addressed Sheahan as 'the respected leader and founder' of the trades association.[89] The motion was carried and it was immediately decided to communicate with O'Connell to ask his advice on how they could best help in returning two repealers.

The response from the trades and mortality societies to these developments was especially encouraging. A representative of the nailors trade union announced that all his members, except three, had declared for repeal while William Ellis, a stonecutter of 47 Douglas Street, said that his trade was entirely for repeal and he took away thirty-nine trades association membership cards for distribution. William Ring similarly informed the association that he had been told that the brogue-makers were for repeal and he had been promised twenty-one of their votes. In fact, by 23 October twenty-five trades societies had met and all had declared for repeal. The trades association drew up a list of another twenty-five to thirty societies and delegates were sent to persuade them to meet. Feargus O'Connor further strengthened the resolve of the association with a rousing speech on repeal at a meeting on 20 October.[90] Baldwin began to attend regularly and on 25 October W.J. O'Neill Daunt, the repeal candidate for Mallow, put in an appearance.[91]

Donegan had commented on 16 October that the new direction would increase their membership 'one-hundred fold'.[92] It is clear that the association had widened its appeal as a result of the policy change and it seems to have firmly established itself as the political voice of the trades of Cork. Moreover, it was being taken seriously by mainstream liberals and, in particular, by radicals like Baldwin and O'Connor. A meeting on 1 November that was attended by Daniel O'Connell himself further enhanced the reputation of the Cork Trades Association. William Ring presided over this packed meeting which heard a lengthy speech from O'Connell stressing the demand for an immediate repeal of the Act of Union: 'Why should we wait awhile? why should we wait any longer? do you, my friends, put off for a month or two, the job that ought to be done tomorrow? why, then, postpone Repeal?'[93]

O'Connell's attendance was a tremendous morale boost for the organisation. However, Sheahan and the tradesmen faced opposition from within the Liberal camp. Baldwin was far from the favourite candidate of the moderate element based in the Chamber of Commerce. In 1830 he had been nominated by James Ludlow Stawell and with the support of many moderate Liberals as well as radicals he had won just 388 votes.[94] Dan Meagher claimed years later that he had early reservations about Baldwin. He seemingly informed the historian, C.B. Gibson, that, 'Mr. Sheahan touched on a point to which I had not been insensible, and I do here confess that *the duelling facility of the Doctor* was always a serious drawback on his merits'.[95] In the election of 1831 Baldwin was pushed to the side and Meagher, James Daly, Charles Beamish, and other moderate Liberals supported Daniel Callaghan.[96] In point of fact, Baldwin was too radical for many in the powerful Chamber of Commerce faction and, worse still, he was not hugely amenable to influence from that direction. Callaghan had first entered parliament in the by-election of March 1830 when he had taken the seat vacated by his Brunswicker younger brother, Gerard. It seemed initially that Daniel (who was a Catholic) was merely a *locum tenens* and he leaned towards Toryism. However, he proved rather Whigish in his politics and soon began to court the moderate Liberals.

Callaghan was heartily distrusted by the trades association, particularly because of his equivocation on the issue of repeal. Sheahan, moreover, reported to a meeting in early November that he had heard that plans were afoot to promote Callaghan as a repealer in order to 'get rid of Baldwin'.[97] He suspected that the limited extension of the franchise allowed by the reform legislation meant that some Liberals felt able to ignore the tradesmen: 'I understand that the Trades Association is thought little of in certain quarters, because the Irish Reform Bill has treated the people with injustice. It has given a vote to but one in every forty of our population. That is a very liberal reason for thinking lightly of the proceedings and sentiments of the great mass of the people!'[98] At the same meeting William Ring, who was a Protestant, lambasted the Chamber of Commerce for its exclusivity and he described the members as 'miserable peacocks' who had betrayed the tradesmen, labourers, and clerks who had raised them 'to office and power'. He declared that his own childrens future prospects lay in 'a knowledge of artisanship' and, in times of unemployment, he believed that the 'nobility of the Chamber' when 'ornamented in the plumage of Aldermanship will put them in the beggar's cart'.[99] Clearly, Ring did not expect the Catholic middle-class Liberals to behave any differently than the Protestant Tories after municipal reform.

In the weeks immediately preceding the election the trades association organised a canvas of the city asking electors to pledge their votes for 'two honest repealers' recommended by the tradesmen.[100] Moreover, they elicited pledges not to accept bribes and actively sought to deter known bribing agents.[101] By early December the number of pledged votes was 1,129.[102] It was soon clear to the Chamber of Commerce faction that they had underestimated the tradesmen and a deputation was despatched from Patrick Street to a trades association meeting called to discuss a public rally at which repeal candidates would be recommended or otherwise. Lyons, Meagher, and Fagan were among the seven-man delegation that made its way to Nelson Place. The meeting was rancorous with both sides berating the other. Meagher, in particular, attacked the trades association for not doing enough to register new voters while William Ring and Richard Dowden made it clear that the association had no intention of endorsing Callaghan unless he unequivocally declared for repeal. The delegation withdrew to shouts of 'Repeal, Repeal, and nothing but Repeal!'[103]

The trades association public meeting was held at the Lancasterian School on 10 December. Thousands attended and both Baldwin and Callaghan turned up to seek the endorsement of the tradesmen. 'It was a happiness and comfort to [my] mind,' declared Cornelius Carver, 'that that body, which originally consisted of but a few unpretending retiring persons, had now assumed a position in the city, second to no public body, for influence, integrity, and independence'. Baldwin's endorsement was not in question but for Callaghan the event was an act of public obsequiousness. Both were required to answer a series of questions before they were deemed acceptable:

SECRETARY: Dr. Baldwin, will you, Sir, vote for a Repeal of the Legislative Union between Great Britain and Ireland?

DR. BALDWIN: I will (*cheering for some time*).

SECRETARY: Will you, Mr. Callaghan?

MR. CALLAGHAN: I will (*repeated cheers*).

SECRETARY: Dr. Baldwin, will you vote for an abolition of Tithes, and of all Church Rates and Cesses?

DR. B.: I will (*cheers*).

SECRETARY: Mr. Callaghan, will you do the same?

MR. C.: I will.

SECRETARY: Dr. Baldwin, will you vote for Triennial Parliaments, a further extension of the Elective Franchise to at least £5 householders, and Vote by Ballot?

DR. B.: I will (*cheers*).

SECRETARY: Mr. Callaghan, will you do the same?

MR. C.: I will.

SECRETARY: Dr. Baldwin, will you vote for the introduction of Jury Bills for Ireland similar to those in England, as well as that of Grand Juries, Municipal Officers, and all Magistrates should be elected by the Rate Payers?

DR. B.: I will (*cheers*).

MR. C.: Certainly (*cheers*).

SECRETARY: Dr. Baldwin, will you vote for the total abolition of Negro Slavery?

DR. B.: Unquestionably (*cheers*).

SECRETARY: Will you, Mr. Callaghan?

MR. C.: I have done so before, and I will do so again with pleasure (*cheers*).

SECRETARY: Dr. Baldwin, will you, Sir, vote for a reduction of all taxes affecting the diffusion of knowledge?

DR. B.: I will (*cheers*).

SECRETARY: Mr. Callaghan?

MR. C.: I will (*cheers*).

SECRETARY: Dr. Baldwin and Mr. Callaghan – Will you, Gentlemen, as Candidates, pledge yourselves that you will not, either by yourselves, or others, directly or indirectly, bribe any of the electors at the ensuing election?

DR. B.: I do most solemnly (*cheers*).

MR. C.: I am delighted to be able to say I will not – (*cheers and laughter*).

MR. DOWDEN: They have said their catechism. Now they may be confirmed (*laughter*).[104]

In fact, Callaghan was subsequently forced to place a newspaper notice to contradict continued rumours that he was not sufficiently committed on repeal.[105] At the conclusion of the public meeting a joint election committee was established representing both the Liberal factions. Sheahan, Ring, Dowden, and others served alongside Meagher, Lyons, Sugrue, Fagan, and other members of the Chamber of Commerce group.

In the event, both Baldwin and Callaghan were elected on 21 December with 2,223 and 2,263 votes respectively. Dan Meagher reneged on the pact arranged on 10 December and he plumped for Callaghan instead of casting a single vote for each of the repeal candidates. This occurred following a heated argument at a committee meeting during polling and it seems that Fagan would have done likewise except that he had already voted. Sheahan exposed Meagher's behaviour in the *Chronicle*.[106] After the votes were counted Callaghan gracefully thanked the trades association for its work. Baldwin was more expansive stating that his time in parliament would be especially directed 'to the improvement of the working mechanic, and of the agricultural labourer, whose condition ... [was] most deplorable'. Furthermore, he confessed that he owed 'his return to the Trades Association, which body he warmly eulogised'.[107] In fact the tradesmen had secured the election of Baldwin despite the machinations of the Chamber of Commerce and had concurrently made the Cork Trades Association a powerful political force in the city.

Repeal and the Cork working class

The Cork city election of 1832 was a tremendous success for the repeal movement and for local Liberalism despite strains within the camp. These internal antagonisms, however, were accentuated in the *Cork Mercantile Chronicle* on 26 December when Thomas Sheahan published two letters from trades association supporters which hinted that they might coalesce with the Conservatives in the next election if mainstream Liberals, and Dan Callaghan's advocates in particular, failed to mend their ways and treat repeal more seriously as a political demand. Both letters lauded Baldwin as 'the real Repeal candidate' while criticising Callaghan, Fagan, and Meagher. As these recriminations were being exercised the election in the county constituency had yet to be decided.

Feargus O'Connor, one of the county repeal candidates, attended a meeting of the Cork Trades Association on 24 December where he received the unambiguous endorsement of the organisation in a motion proposed by Sheahan. Herbert Baldwin lavishly praised O'Connor and remarked that the Catholics of Cork were obliged to vote for him as a repayment of 'the debt of gratitude' owed to his uncle, the leading United Irishman, Arthur O'Connor, who was then living in exile in France. Feargus O'Connor ran on a radical platform, demanding annual parliaments among other advanced measures, but he was also apt to enhance himself with references to his famous uncle.[1] 'The learned Doctor [Baldwin],' he declared at the trades association meeting, 'told you I was the nephew of the Arthur O'Connor who sooner than sell Ireland forfeited sixteen thousand a year. I glory in his sacrifice, and my greatest boast shall be to imitate his example'.[2] In the event, O'Connor and another less reliable repealer, Garrett Standish Barry, were returned in the county.[3] O'Connor topped the poll with 1,837 votes causing increased delight among Cork radicals. One of those who had a vote in this election was the leading socialist, William Thompson, who owned an estate in west Cork. Unfortunately, the poll books no longer exist but it is plausible to assume that Thompson would have voted for the future Chartist, Feargus O'Connor, which, if proved, would make an interesting historical conjunction.

The trades association decided to celebrate its success with a formal 'chairing' of the two city members of parliament despite objections from Richard Dowden and James Hayes that such triumphalism would 'needlessly hurt the feelings of the conquered Tories'.[4] The tradesmen outvoted the middle-class radical members on the issue and a demonstration was advertised for New Year's Day 1833. Thousands assembled for the event, which was entirely organised by the trades association and included at least twenty-two of the city's trades. The Chamber of Commerce faction did not involve itself. Led by three musical bands (from the trades association, the weavers, and the victuallers) Baldwin and Callaghan were brought in procession at 1.30 p.m. from the Lancasterian School on Lancaster Quay. They first moved eastwards along New Street (now Washington Street), then southwards across Clarke's bridge, up Fitton Street, Bishop Street, Brandy Lane, Maypole Lane, down Barrack Street, along the South and North Main Streets to the North Gate bridge where they temporarily halted. 'All along this line of march,' reported the *Chronicle*, 'the windows, doors, and the house-tops were occupied by men, women, and children, saluting the "two Repealers," and saluted by them in turn'.[5]

At the North Gate bridge William Ring read an open letter to the MPs signed by two women, Mary Connell and Mary Murphy, pleading on behalf of the destitute of the northern parishes:

> Be assured that your duty is to relieve soon and permanently, this immense mass of destitution . . . Your fellow-citizens have told you that a Repeal of the Union alone can greatly benefit Ireland. To the effecting of that Repeal, we exhort, we entreat you by our rags, by our hunger – by the sufferings we have felt, and those which we now endure.[6]

Following a march through the northside districts the demonstration moved into Patrick Street in the city-centre and back to the Lancasterian School where both members of parliament made speeches in which they promised to do something for the poor of the city. Ring also reiterated the message that he had delivered at the North Gate bridge and he called on Baldwin and Callaghan to 'pull together'. In fact, while the trades association 'chairing' was a victory celebration it was also clearly intended to emphasise the urgent desire for repeal in working-class Cork. Moreover, the politicians were brought on a tour of some of the poorest districts in the city in a blunt effort to remind them of the level of destitution that pervaded those areas. The cholera epidemic had still not fully run its course and the poor, who lived in especially congested conditions, remained its most common victims.

In the wake of the election the Cork Trades Association passed a motion praising the work of its secretary, John Creedon, and a formal address was presented to twenty-seven-year-old Francis Bernard Beamish thanking him for his services to the organisation.[7] The tradesmen particularly cherished Beamish, a Protestant and a member of an important brewing family, because, in a hierarchical world, he added to the respectability of the association. 'We are called democrats,' claimed a member, 'and so we are; yet . . . we have amongst us – rank, and wealth, and influence, and connexion, united with

2. Begging in Cork in the early nineteenth century
(from A.M. and S.C. Hall, *Ireland: its scenery, character, etc.* vol. 1, London, 1841)

honesty, virtue, and patriotism'.[8] In fact, the Cork Trades Association seems to have attracted a substantial number of the city's Protestant Liberals. Among those involved were Beamish, William Crawford jun., Richard Dowden, Isaac Varian, and William Ring. Some of these, like Dowden and Ring, were undoubtedly political radicals but the same cannot be said for Frank Beamish who in later years was rather lukewarm on repeal although he was a strong advocate of municipal reform.[9] Beamish was politically ambitious and he was interested in entering parliament. It is probable that Protestant Liberals found the Catholic-dominated Chamber of Commerce a cold house. In post-emancipation Ireland Catholic merchants and manufacturers like Fagan, Meagher and Lyons were unlikely to quell their own political ambitions to facilitate a Protestant parliamentary candidate. When Francis B. Beamish was elected as an MP for the city in 1837 it was with the support of the base that he had built around the trades association. Indeed, from 1833 he acted almost like its official patron and he was soon made president of the organisation.

Thomas Sheahan also received plaudits from the tradesmen who organised a banquet in his honour on 18 February 1833. Two hundred people, mostly working class, sat down to a dinner which was presided over by Charles Sugrue who reminded them of Sheahan's struggle against the magistrates of Clonakilty in 1824. He went on to credit Sheahan with 'ridding the City of that moral plague of bribery and corruption' during the recent election and with 'fostering' the trades association. In his reply Thomas Sheahan pointedly attacked recent coercive legislation and he called for working class unity on the issue of repeal:

> Let but the feeling of brotherhood which is diffusing itself among the oppressed working classes of the people of Ireland, both Catholic and Protestant, extend itself a little more, and the Repeal is carried (cheers). I here tell the enemies of Ireland that they miscalculate if they think that the Catholics and Protestants of this country will be always at variance. Is it to be supposed that they are insensible to every thing that is passing around them?[10]

This appeal to Protestants was formalised at a trades association meeting held three days later when it was agreed to draw up an *Appeal to the operative Protestants of the City and County of Cork* 'on the subject of their conditions as working men, and on their duties as Irishmen'.[11] A Protestant hosier named Nutty spoke in support of this appeal and he denounced the Act of Union which he claimed had reduced the number of hosiers in the city from 300 to less than thirty of whom only nine or ten had steady employment.

Unfortunately, the association's efforts to reach out to Protestant workers received a serious setback some weeks later with the death of Sheahan's close friend and political ally, William Ring.[12] Unlike Beamish, who generally only presided at meetings or lent his name, Ring was an activist and a central figure in the day-to-day running of the organisation. Moreover, he was an Episcopalian Protestant from a staunchly unionist background who had embraced repeal and, in addition, he was a man who had an easy rapport with ordinary workers. Ring was born in 1796 in the Shandon weigh-house where his father, Thomas, had been weighmaster for many years. Following his father's death in 1804 the family moved to 3 Mary Street in the south of the city where his mother established a pawnbroking business. Thomas Ring had been Adjutant of the City of Cork Militia and the Rings were solidly conservative and unionist in their politics.[13] It seems that William's advocacy of repeal and tithe abolition came as something of a shock to many old family acquaintances.

Ring, who lived in Mallow Lane, had spent time in the pawnbroking business before establishing a small distillery in Blackpool on the northside of the city. This distillery, which was worked by an overshot waterwheel rather than a steam engine, was the smallest in the city producing just 500 pancheons of whiskey per season. Andy Bielenberg has calculated that it produced only 0.8 per cent of the city output in 1828.[14] By early 1832 Ring's distilling venture was in trouble and he placed advertisements seeking capital investment.[15] This failed to materialise and his business collapsed leaving his family in significant financial distress. With the outbreak of the cholera epidemic, however, he was appointed to a paid position as officer of health for the Shandon parish of St

Anne's and for the following twelve months he was engaged in combating the disease. Likewise, he played a central role in both the Irish Manufacture Association and the Cork Trades Association as well as being a vigorous advocate of repeal. He was a popular individual who took the radical side in local politics and it is clear that the demise of his own fortunes caused him to seriously reassess his political outlook. Sheahan felt that political opponents sometimes used this against him:

> Some low-minded Liberals, jealous of the fame which he was every day acquiring, and chagrined because the public did not make demi-gods of their nothingness – were in the habit of saying that, indeed, they had not heard of Mr. Ring until the world went against him. Contemptible things, they forgot in the malice of their breasts that providence ordains adversity for the greater manifestation of the virtues of some men; and that there are those who are worthless in every turn of life. While these Liberals were gnawing away his reputation, more than one Conservative was engaged in proclaiming that he had become a Revolutionist, that he had thrown himself body and soul into the hands of the Catholics, and that he was ready to employ fire and sword to promote the objects of his new allies . . . [For] the poor, for Irish Manufactures, and Repeal, William Ring would have laid down his life.[16]

In a sense he did. On the morning of 23 March 1833 he fell ill to cholera and by 1.30 p.m. the following day he was dead, leaving behind a pregnant wife and six young children. The members of the trades association were shocked by this unexpected death and there was a large attendance at Ring's funeral despite the fact that he had died of cholera.[17] He was buried in the graveyard of St Anne's, Shandon, which was only a few yards from where he was born. In 1834 the Cork Trades Association erected an obelisk-type monument over his grave on which inscriptions panegyrised him as a 'friend of the poor', a 'zealous Repealer', and a 'promoter of Irish manufactures'. This monument, neglected and long-forgotten, stands today beneath a large tree in the overgrown southern section of Shandon graveyard (fig. 3).

William Ring was scarcely buried before the Cork Trades Association found itself facing another crisis. The cause this time lay far from the cholera-ravaged streets of Shandon. In the election of 1832 Daniel O'Connell had fought to make repeal the primary issue and the outcome was the return of thirty-nine Irish MPs determined to demand the retraction of the Act of Union.[18] Cork had sent two especially vigorous repealers, Herbert Baldwin and Feargus O'Connor, to Westminster and action was expected. However, O'Connell soon began to vacillate in his dealings with the whig government despite its introduction of extremely severe coercion measures which he strongly resisted.[19] This repressive legislation became law in early April and

3. Cork Trades Association memorial to William Ring (1796–1833) in Shandon graveyard

was prompted by the heightened tithe and repeal agitation in Ireland. It appalled Irish repealers and the Cork Trades Association fully expected to be banned under its strictures.[20] That did not happen. Instead, in March 1833 Edward Stanley, the aggressive Irish chief secretary, shifted to another post and this served to mollify O'Connell slightly. He developed a workable relation-ship with the new incumbent and, moreover, decided that the time was not yet right for bringing a motion on repeal before parliament.[21]

The Cork tradesmen had sent a petition on repeal to Westminster and Herbert Baldwin was entrusted with bringing it to the attention of the govern-ment. On 10 April he appeared at a trades association meeting and explained that O'Connell had advised him against presenting the Cork petition while the coercion bill was being discussed. The tradesmen instructed Baldwin to bring the question of repeal before the house of commons at the earliest possible opportunity.[22] However, O'Connell continued to oppose the intro-duction of a repeal debate, fearing an inglorious defeat and the unnecessary upset of his relations with the government, and Feargus O'Connor eventually openly denounced his behaviour. O'Connell tried to outflank O'Connor by convening a meeting of repeal MPs at which his waiting policy was backed. This was not a complete success as at the meeting on 10 June O'Connell won by a mere twelve votes to ten, with ten abstentions.[23] In Cork the trades association heard of Feargus O'Connor's move with great excitement and entirely supported his position.[24] Indeed, Sheahan was not in the least dismayed by O'Connor's defeat at the Irish parliamentary party meeting:

> I look upon this division as entirely favourable to what I believe to be the wish of this Association – immediate discussion. There were several persons in the majority, sons or sons-in-law of Mr. O'Connell, who could not well avoid adopting the views of that gentleman; in a word, I consider the advocates for immediate discussion as having had a virtual majority (*hear, hear*).[25]

Baldwin, who was backing Feargus O'Connor, was again urged to push forward with repeal when he wrote to the Cork Trades Association requesting fresh instructions. On 13 June, while arguing in support of O'Connor, Sheahan underlined the heterogeneous nature of the nationalist movement:

> There is a prejudice abroad that Mr. O'Connell's general supporters are a mere mob – a herd of animals without any mind of their own – who move at his bidding, whether it be wise or whether it be foolish – who adopt all his whims and schemes, and are ready to execute them, be they good or ill. We are supposed by many to be a portion of this herd – and hence our voice has not the influence to which it is entitled, nor Mr. O'Connell the weight to which our cool deliberate attachment ought to give him. Rely on it, gentlemen, that the vote to which, I trust, you will come this evening will, though not in accordance with Mr. O'Connell's judgement, but strengthen the hands of that gentleman. It will teach the Government that Mr. O'Connell is not the

only repealer – that he is backed in Ireland by millions of repealers who reflect on the merits of the question, and form opinions for themselves, as to the proper mode of advancing it – that he is backed by millions of reasoning men (*hear, hear, hear*).[26]

The meeting of the trades association unanimously endorsed O'Connor and Baldwin with nobody offering to speak in support of O'Connell.

Feargus O'Connor placed a repeal motion before parliament on 16 July without first informing O'Connell who then hinted that he might disavow the proponents and merely stand by in the debate. Realising the damage that this would do O'Connor ultimately withdrew his motion on the day that it was due to be discussed. O'Connell, meanwhile, assured the repeal movement that he would raise the issue at the next session of parliament in 1834. He had not intended to do so but was forced into this promise by the intense pressure he had endured. In Dublin Patrick O'Higgins, Patrick Lavelle (of the *Freeman's Journal*), and Thomas Reynolds had also raised an agitation for immediate discussion and on 19 June, some time after the Cork Trades Association had adopted its stance, they carried a motion at a parish meeting of St Audeon's that greatly alarmed O'Connell and his associates.[27] According to Fergus D'Arcy, however, Dublin tradesmen in general appear to have remained on reasonably good terms with O'Connell until as late as April 1834.[28]

Daniel O'Connell was not quickly forgiven in Cork for his attempts to postpone debate on repeal. At a public dinner held in his honour in the rooms of the Cork Chamber of Commerce on 4 November his less than staunch comments on repeal led to a series of critical and embarrassing interjections from Feargus O'Connor. O'Connor then followed his 'leader' with a speech in which he called on Irishmen to demand 'repeal, the whole repeal, and nothing but repeal'.[29] It was clear that O'Connell was being warned against further vacillation but the Lichfield House compact of 1835 later indicated his propensity for collaboration with Whig governments.

Thomas Sheahan continued to promote repeal in the columns of the *Cork Mercantile Chronicle* until he resigned as editor in late 1833, possibly to concentrate on the family business in Dominick Street.[30] In November he published his second book which he titled *Articles of Irish manufacture; or portions of Cork history*. It was essentially a compilation of letters, articles, sketches, and other pieces that he had written between 1824 and 1832 but it also included some commentary, introductions, and footnotes that provide interesting material for the historian of local Cork politics. In the same month he issued another publication – *An address to such tradesmen of Cork as compose the Cork 'Union of Trades'* – and this short polemic is a most useful source in terms of understanding his attitude to trade unionism. Only 500 copies were printed but the *Address to tradesmen* was also published in full on the front page of the *Chronicle*.[31]

The occasion for Sheahan's polemic was an upsurge in labour violence in the course of 1833. Trade unions were effectively illegal before 1824 as a result of the Combination Acts but that did not prevent workers, particularly tradesmen, from establishing localised unions, or societies, or from engaging in collective action.[32] In the early 1820s, for instance, there was a wave of violent attacks on employers, strikebreakers, and on the property of offending individuals. Many of the city trades united in 1820 in a 'Cork Union of Trades' and this underground trades council was responsible for co-ordinating local labour disputes.[33] It organised funds to sustain strikers, it bore the expenses of providing lawyers for arrested labour activists, and on occasion it bought off witnesses in court cases. Most controversially, it was associated with at least eight murders during 1820–1.[34] In general, the *modus operandi* was that if a trade struck the violent attacks on employers and strikebreakers would be carried out by an entirely separate section of the Union of Trades. In other words, if the coopers were in dispute, the men who arrived to assault the errant employer were most likely shoemakers or tailors but rarely the coopers themselves. The coopers, in turn, would later repay the favour if one of the other trades required assistance.[35]

This first Cork Union of Trades collapsed in late 1821. It seems that financial difficulties were the cause of its demise though Thomas Sheahan also suggested that another factor might have been a dispute between the shoemakers and the broguemakers.[36] A second Union of Trades emerged in the early 1830s and it too was associated with an upsurge of labour violence in the city. The trade unions still operated in a furtive manner, despite decriminalisation, and many disguised themselves as mortality or friendly societies. There were efforts made to link the trades and labourers societies to the Cork Trades Association but, in reality, they served rather different functions. The local unions (often called 'combinations') were essentially working class defence mechanisms whose main concerns were wage-rates and working conditions. The Cork Union of Trades existed to strengthen the workers' position during labour disputes. The Cork Trades Association, on the other hand, was primarily a working class political organisation that looked towards a larger picture. It aimed to halt de-industrialisation in Cork city by restoring the national parliament. Sheahan and his friends believed that only a repeal of the Act of Union could bring prosperity to working-class Cork. They also believed that labour and agrarian violence retarded the struggle for repeal. Both the Cork Union of Trades and the Cork Trades Association represented local tradesmen but in different spheres.

In January 1833 violent assaults during a slaters dispute presaged the temper of the year.[37] On 4 March a crowd of over 100 masons assembled at midnight near Evergreen Cross from where they marched to the property of W. H. W. Newenham at Sheabeg and pulled down a wall that he had recently erected. Labourers rather than masons had built the wall.[38] Convictions occurred as a result of this incident but that did not deter other labour activists. The rest of 1833 saw a spate of such episodes. In June, for example, Dominick Street was affected when during a coopers dispute a mob descended on a cooperage that was being used to store empty firkins and set it on fire. The same group had earlier attacked the house of a cooper named Sullivan in Clarence Street smashing his doors and windows with stones.[39] By November Sheahan was worried that the aggressive tactics being utilised would lead to deaths as had happened in 1820–1. His *Address to tradesmen* pleaded with them to avoid murder and to abandon the Union of Trades: 'I say you are no Repealers, long as you remain Union of Trades men, with your present principles. Madness, to think of carrying Repeal, whilst you are cutting each others throats!'[40] He explicitly compared them with the whiteboys and suggested that they offended against both God and humanity.

Sheahan made a number of recommendations in his polemic on how trade unionists should operate. First, he told them that they must give up all secret meetings, organise in the open, and 'appeal to public opinion for support – you being on the right side'. Secondly, during labour disputes they should assist in establishing neutral 'arbitration juries' that would decide on the merits of the issues. Also, they should take the advice of the trades association and involve themselves in the campaign for repeal. Finally, he argued that,

> I would have you . . . to petition for a legal provision for the poor. Is a man to starve when his employer tells him that he can no longer give him work at the usual terms? No, he will offer to work for less and not starve: do not you murder him for doing so. Strive rather that the right of public provision in the hour of necessity be secured by law to the poor man in Ireland, as it is secured to him in England. Succeed in that . . . and your fellow tradesman, then, in his time of need, instead of coming in on your bone, which is little enough for yourself, will fall back on the public table, and partake of it, till he can better his condition.[41]

Sheahan was also very critical of the apprenticeship system which he believed was an exclusionary practice. However, the central thrust of his appeal was undoubtedly against the use of violence in labour disputes.

It had little impact and violent incidents continued. Pistols were used during a stonecutters dispute in early December and a mob of tailors tried to drag a merchant from his carriage later in the month. In fact, the incidents became almost nightly occurrences during November and December with houses ransacked and their inhabitants badly beaten. As a result of these labour disturbances a police force was introduced into Cork city for the first time to replace the plainly ineffective watch system.[42] The new force ultimately failed to stop the violence and outrages continued to occur through 1834 and 1835.[43] Indeed, in 1835 the local trade unionists added vitriol (sulphuric acid) to their repertoire and a number of employers and strikebreakers were seriously injured. The face was commonly the target and eyes were regularly lost.[44] Sheahan denounced the throwing of vitriol in February 1835 as a 'hell born act'.[45]

During 1834 Thomas Sheahan and the trades association continued to vigorously campaign for repeal and the abolition of tithes.[46] Also, in March 1834 both he and Edward Donegan, the weaver, were among those who gave evidence before the Royal Commission for Inquiring into the Condition of the Poorer Classes in Ireland when it sat in Cork.[47] He subsequently published his evidence, with an introduction and footnotes, as a pamphlet, *Irish destitution in 1834; or the working classes of Cork* (1834). One interesting argument that he put to the Irish poor inquiry was that men from depressed trades were actually worse off than labourers because they were less attuned to poverty. In other words, labourers had developed stratagems for dealing with low wage-rates and poor conditions while tradesmen, who were used to better, found their reduced circumstances difficult to deal with and were more likely to turn to drink.[48]

In October the trades association organised a huge demonstration to welcome the English reformer and MP, William Cobbett, to Cork.[49] Thousands of people, led by Baldwin, Sheahan, Creedon, O'Donovan and other Cork Trades Association leaders, met Cobbett as he approached the city and brought him in procession to a rally outside the Chamber of Commerce on Patrick Street. Cobbett, who was on a tour of Ireland, gave three lectures while in Cork, the last of which directly addressed the issue of repeal.[50] At this time, Feargus O'Connor was especially active in the county and city on the issue of repeal and tithes, and in the general election of January 1835 he was easily returned to parliament. However, a petition was immediately brought against him by the Tories and his election was declared invalid because he did not fulfil the requisite property qualification.[51] O'Connor subsequently exported his political energy to Britain where he became the leading figure in the radical Chartist movement. In Cork city the tradesmen suffered disappointment when Baldwin lost his seat in 1835 but the trades association nonetheless remained an influential force in local politics.[52] Baldwin subsequently regained the seat on petition.

Sheahan, meanwhile, lobbied against the duty on glass in 1834 and 1835 arguing that it was responsible for the poor state of the local glass manufacturing industry.[53] He also lambasted the city's pawnbrokers and in December 1835 he sent open letters to Baldwin and Callaghan, who had been re-installed as the Cork MPs, asking them to promote a system of *Mont de Piété* as a substitute for traditional pawnshops.[54] This system allowed loans of small sums at a nominal rate of interest to people who would otherwise be forced to borrow from usurers. It was essentially an argument for public loanshops with some similarities to present-day credit unions. Sheahan himself did not have the finances to establish such a venture and it seems that his efforts to involve others were ultimately unsuccessful.

From February 1835 the central project of the Cork Trades Association was the erection of a 'People's Hall'.[55] Cornelius Carver explained that the proposed building would be a bastion against conservatism and a political focal point for radicals and O'Connellites. In fact, it was to provide a physical and political alternative to the Chamber of Commerce. Sheahan, who seems to have been the prime mover behind the hall, declared,

> The Peoples Hall would be erected on the broadest principles – it would be no sectarian institution, neither Protestant nor Catholic, nor rich, nor poor, should have an exclusive right to it, but as the poor were the greatest in number, their interests should occupy most of its attention.[56]

It was also suggested that the trades association rename itself as the 'People's Association' in order to broaden its membership but this proposal, which threatened the dominance of the tradesmen, was not adopted.[57] In August the association briefly diverted itself from the People's Hall project to organise a 'grand entry' into the city for the new lord lieutenant.[58] The earl of Mulgrave, who had been appointed in April, was a reformer who enjoyed the respect of the O'Connellite party and the trades of Cork were eager to show their appreciation of his conciliatory policy.[59]

Thomas Sheahan did not live to see the completion of the People's Hall. On 29 March 1836 he died at his home in Dominick Street of 'malignant fever'. The Cork Trades Association hurriedly summoned an emergency meeting for the following evening 'to adopt the best means of testifying their great respect, as well as universal sorrow, for their founder Mr. Sheahan'.[60] It was an unhappy gathering. The *Southern Reporter* noted that the members 'private feeling' was 'so excited' that no resolution could be formulated though a committee was appointed to arrange the funeral. It was also agreed to hold another meeting to discuss the erection of a suitable monument to 'the poor man's friend'.[61]

Sheahan's funeral on 1 April was an elaborate affair. The procession left 25 Dominick Street led by eight Catholic clergymen, walking two abreast, after whom came the hearse, bearing a richly ornamented coffin, with three bearers on either side. The chief mourners included his mother, Catherine Sheahan, Francis Bernard Beamish, and William Crawford. Behind them was a long train of mourners, accompanied by the trades of the city, who carried poles tipped with black crape and white lace. The pedestrian mourners were in turn followed by carriages and other vehicles in a procession that was described a 'great concourse'.[62] It slowly made its way along Pope's Quay, across Patrick's bridge, up Patrick Street, the Grand Parade, over Parliament bridge, and towards Evergreen Cross. Sheahan was buried in the new Catholic

4. St Joseph's cemetery in the late 1830s (from Hall's *Ireland etc.* vol. 1)

graveyard, St Joseph's, which Fr Theobold Mathew had recently established on the site of the old botanic gardens (fig. 4). There was a deep religiosity to the affair which aptly reflected Sheahan's strong adhesion to his religion. According to the *Southern Reporter*:

> The solemnity of the scene was deep and impressive, there broke upon the ear, the intonation of the psalm *Miserere*. The voices of the priests were now raised, and the chant proceeded in four harmonized parts. The sounds blended admirably, the melody was full, the effect was deep. And to those that knew him, who was the object of this last tribute of respect, from a body of men who had looked upon him as one of themselves, it seemed like the welcome of his pure spirit into those regions 'where the weary shall be at rest, and the wicked shall cease from troubling'.[63]

At a meeting of the trades association on 11 April it was decided to build a substantial monument on Sheahan's grave. A committee was established to organise this which included many of his friends and political allies like Frank Beamish, Frank Walsh, Edward Lane, Cornelius Carver, Richard Dowden, Daniel Casey, Charles Sugrue, and James J. Hayes. A particular appeal was made to the trades of the city to contribute to the cost of the memorial.[64] In the event, the Cork Trades Association erected a magnificent monument to its founder with inscriptions in English, Irish and Ogham. It stands as testimony to the respect and popularity that Thomas Sheahan enjoyed in his native city.

Conclusion

Thomas Sheahan was never a national figure and even in Cork city he was only one in a group of leading figures that helped to shape local nationalist politics in the 1820s and 1830s. He was, however, different from most within this group in the sense that his primary motivation was the elimination of social destitution rather than the elevation of Liberalism or, indeed, the Catholic middle class. He was moved, according to an obituarist in the *Southern Reporter*, by 'his strict moral virtue, his deep sense of religion, and his untiring sympathies for the poor'. The same writer opined that Sheahan may have 'miscalculated' his aptitude for public life because he 'was too earnest, too single-minded and too uncompromising, not to startle at times the common herd of politicians'.[1]

There is some truth in this statement but it is also an underestimation of Sheahan's political acuity. The politicians that he startled were undoubtedly those nestled in the comfort of the Chamber of Commerce and it is clear that he contrived to jolt these individuals. On the issue of repeal, in common with the tradesmen, he was uncompromising and unlikely to accept the arguments of more orthodox O'Connellites. Indeed, the example of the Cork Trades Association accentuates the ambiguous value of 'O'Connellism' as a shorthand term to describe the nationalist movement of that period. Was Thomas Sheahan an 'O'Connellite'? This can only be tentatively answered. He was, insofar as he generally accepted the political leadership of Daniel O'Connell, but he clearly believed that the repeal movement, for example, was larger than O'Connell and that commentators were mistaken in presuming that the 'Liberator' led an unreflective mob.

Sheahan was enormously concerned by the de-industrialisation that he observed in certain sectors of the local economy. Initially he had hoped that a campaign to promote Irish manufactures would have some positive impact but he soon identified repeal as the social panacea that he was seeking. This perspective was shared by many Cork tradesmen who blamed the Act of Union for the social misery that stalked their city. He was also clear in understanding the necessity for tradesmen to obtain some form of political power in order to advance towards their objectives. Indeed, one of Sheahan's criticisms of trade unionism was its focus on defensive measures and its unwillingness to take political initiatives. In 1835 he commented negatively on the British unions at a meeting of the trades association:

Universal suffrage was one of the objects he [Sheahan] sought to gain, and would be that, he was certain, of every gentleman in the Association. Without political power it was vain to think life, liberty, and property, could be protected. The Trades Unions of England, [and] Scotland would have done much better if, instead of pursuing Owenite doctrines, they had directed their intelligence, good feeling, funds, and power, to the attainment of political strength, by the constitutional exertion of which, they would not be trusting to two or three representatives of the labouring classes in the present Parliament but ... very probably have from twenty to thirty members to support them![2]

This is almost the language of Chartism and there can be no doubt of Sheahan's political radicalism. This makes him something other than a simple philanthropist. He believed that the working class should have direct access to political power.

The Cork Trades Association did gain a modicum of political power in the influence that it was able to exert locally during elections. However, the organisation quickly became a gathering place for a number of disaffected middle-class radicals and the trades influence was modified by that of these more affluent members who often had different priorities. Francis Bernard Beamish certainly used the tradesmen as a political base for his own ambitions. His patronage was ultimately responsible for the building of the People's Hall at the corner of Castle Street and the North Main Street in 1837. This hall did serve for many years as a nationalist alternative to the Chamber of Commerce and it was the focal point for Cork radicalism until the late 1840s. The Cork Trades Association, which seemingly survived until the early 1850s, eventually abandoned the People's Hall in 1847 when the Young Irelanders effectively took control of the premises.[3] The building was later bought in the 1850s by the Cork Catholic Young Men's Society and today it operates as a scout hall.[4] All traces of the trades association have long disappeared.

Thomas Sheahan was one of hundreds of local leaders who built the infrastructure of the Irish nationalist movement of the 1820s and 1830s. His activity rarely reached outside his native place and he had an especial connection to the Dominick Street area of Cork city. Indeed, his chief concern often seems to have been his own immediate locality. In that sense he is probably representative of many more who were equally committed but much less prominent.

Notes

ABBREVIATIONS

CC	*The Constitution* (or *Cork Constitution*)
CAI	Cork Archives Institute
CEH	*Cork Evening Herald*
CMC	*Cork Mercantile Chronicle*
CSORP	Chief Secretary's Office Registered Papers
NA	National Archives
NLI	National Library of Ireland
PP	*People's Press*
SR	*Southern Reporter*

INTRODUCTION

1 Fergus O'Ferrall, *Daniel O'Connell* (Dublin, 1981) p. 13.

2 John Windele, *Historical and descriptive notices of the city of Cork and its vicinity* (Cork, 1846 edition) pp 139–40.

3 Fergus O'Ferrall, *Catholic emancipation: Daniel O'Connell and the birth of Irish democracy, 1820–1830* (Dublin, 1985); Oliver MacDonagh, *The hereditary bondsman: Daniel O'Connell, 1775–1829* (London, 1989).

4 Thomas Bartlett, *The fall and rise of the Irish nation: the Catholic question, 1690–1830* (Dublin, 1992) pp 327–47.

EARLY YEARS

1 Sheahan's age at death is given on the monument mentioned in the 'Introduction'. For his parents see, *Connor's Cork directory for the year 1817* (Cork, 1817) p. 78 and *SR* 9 April 1836. A search of Roman Catholic records for his baptism registration was unsuccessful which is scarcely unusual for the period involved. The family, incidentally, sometimes spelled the name as 'Shehane'.

2 *CMC* 15 Nov. 1833; Thomas Sheahan, *Irish destitution in 1834; or the working classes of Cork* (Cork, 1834) p. 12.

3 *Pigot's City of Dublin and Hibernian Provincial Directory for 1824* (London, 1824) p. 249.

4 *SR* 9 April 1836; *List of the freemen and freeholders, alphabetically arranged, who voted at the Cork election, December 1826* (Cork, 1827) p. 97.

5 Sheahan, *Irish destitution in 1834*, p. 12.

6 Colman O'Mahony, *In the shadows: life in Cork, 1750–1930* (Cork, 1997) p. 43.

7 On the fever and employment crises of late 1816 to 1819, see O'Mahony, *In the shadows*, pp 86–94; and William Harty, *A historic sketch of the causes, progress, extent, and mortality of the contagious fever epidemic in Ireland during the years 1817, 1818 and 1819* (Dublin, 1820).

8 *First report of the royal commission into the condition of the poorer classes in Ireland. Appendix C – Part I. State of the poor and charitable institutions in principal towns*, H.C. 1836, [35], xxx, p. 24.

9 *Pigot's directory for 1824*, pp 248–9.

10 Colin Rynne, *At the sign of the cow: the Cork butter market, 1770–1924* (Cork, 1998) pp 42–72; Maura Cronin, *Country, class or craft?: The politicisation of the skilled artisan in nineteenth-century Cork* (Cork, 1994) p. 32; William O'Sullivan, *The economic history of Cork city from the earliest times to the act of union* (Cork, 1937) pp 256–79.

11 Windele, *Historical and descriptive notices*, p. 139.
12 Gearóid Ó Tuathaigh, *Ireland before the Famine, 1798–1848* (Dublin, 1972) pp 57–8.
13 Sean Connolly, *Priests and people in pre-Famine Ireland, 1780–1845* (Dublin, 1982) pp 35–43.
14 *SR* 31 March 1836.
15 Thomas Sheahan, *Articles of Irish manufacture; or portions of Cork history* (Cork, 1833) p. 9. For Deasy's residence see, *Pigot's directory for 1824*, p. 235.
16 James Coombes, *Utopia in Glandore* (Butlerstown, 1970) p. 8.
17 O'Ferrall, *Catholic emancipation*, p. 37.
18 O'Ferrall, *Catholic emancipation*, p. 38.
19 Ó Tuathaigh, *Ireland before the Famine*, p. 62.
20 Sheahan, *Articles of Irish manufacture*, p. 9.
21 Sheahan, *Articles of Irish manufacture*, p. 8.
22 *Cork Advertiser*, 4 May 1824, quoted in Sheahan, *Articles of Irish manufacture*, pp 9–10.
23 *Weekly Dublin Satirist*, 21 March 1835; *PP* 28 March 1835.
24 Sheahan, *Articles of Irish manufacture*, pp 10–11.
25 Sheahan, *Articles of Irish manufacture*, p. 10.
26 Thomas Sheahan, *Excursions from Bandon in the south of Ireland by a plain Englishman* (London, 1825) p. 89.
27 Sheahan, *Articles of Irish manufacture*, pp 11–25.
28 Sheahan, *Articles of Irish manufacture*, p. 27.
29 Sheahan, *Articles of Irish manufacture*, p. 28.
30 Sheahan, *Articles of Irish manufacture*, pp 30–1.
31 *Dublin Evening Post*, 10 August 1824.
32 O'Ferrall, *Catholic emancipation*, p. 114.
33 Sheahan, *Articles of Irish manufacture*, pp 31–4.
34 O'Ferrall, *Daniel O'Connell*, p. 57.
35 Sheahan, *Excursions from Bandon*, p. 92.
36 Sheahan, *Excursions from Bandon*, p. 9.
37 Sheahan, *Excursions from Bandon*, p. 34.
38 Sheahan, *Excursions from Bandon*, pp 12–14.
39 Sheahan, *Excursions from Bandon*, p. 102.

40 Sheahan, *Excursions from Bandon*, pp 74, 20–1, 25–30, 28.
41 Sheahan, *Articles of Irish manufacture*, p. 28.
42 Sheahan, *Excursions from Bandon*, pp 94, 98.
43 *CMC* 20 August 1828.
44 Sheahan, *Excursions from Bandon*, p. 85.
45 Sheahan, *Excursions from Bandon*, pp 88–9.
46 Sheahan, *Excursions from Bandon*, p. 88.
47 Sheahan, *Excursions from Bandon*, pp 55–56; O'Ferrall, *Daniel O'Connell*, pp 49–50.
48 Joseph Lee, 'Capital in the Irish economy' in L.M Cullen (ed.), *The formation of the Irish economy* (Cork, 1969) pp 58–9.
49 Sheahan, *Excursions from Bandon*, pp 65, 74, 107, 109–111.

DEMANDING DEMOCRACY

1 Sheahan, *Articles of Irish manufacture*, p. 34.
2 *SR* 14, 18 January 1826; *CC* 14, 24 January 1826.
3 *CC* 17, 24 January 1826; *SR* 2 February, 13 April 1826.
4 *SR* 15 June 1826.
5 *SR* 13 July 1826; *CMC* 9 August 1826. On the situation in Dublin, also see David O'Toole, 'The employment crisis of 1826', in David Dickson (ed.), *The gorgeous mask: Dublin, 1700–1850* (Dublin, 1987) pp 157–172.
6 Henry Goulburn to Thomas Harrison, 7 September 1826 published in *CC* 12 September 1826 and *SR* 9 September 1826.
7 Quoted in Thomas Sheahan, 'Poor Laws in Ireland' in *Irish Catholic Magazine*, July 1829, p. 157. On Gerard Callaghan and the poor laws, also see *CC* 24 August 1826; *CMC* 25 August 1826.
8 *CC* 19 August 1826.
9 *Freeman's Journal* 25 August 1826.
10 *CMC* 18, 21 August 1826.
11 *CC* 9 September 1826.
12 Sheahan, 'Poor Laws in Ireland', pp 153–69.
13 Sheahan, *Irish destitution in 1834*, p. ix.

14 On Thompson, see Richard Pankhurst, *William Thompson, 1775–1833* (London, 1954) and Dolores Dooley, *Equality in community: sexual equality in the writings of William Thompson and Anna Doyle Wheeler* (Cork, 1996).

15 *SR* 29 August 1826; *CC* 31 August 1826.

16 *SR* 22, 26 August 1826.

17 Dooley, *Equality in community*, pp 34–35.

18 Fintan Lane, *The origins of modern Irish socialism* (Cork, 1997) pp 7–10; Robert Owen, *Mr. Owen's plan for the amelioration of the population of Ireland, illustrated by statements and calculations proving the practicability of such an amelioration affording permanent security to the possessors of every description of property in Ireland* (Dublin, 1822).

19 *SR* 15, 17 August 1826.

20 John B. O'Brien, *The Catholic middle classes in Pre-Famine Cork* (Dublin, 1979) pp 19–20.

21 *Copy of instructions given by the Chief Secretary for Ireland with reference to the cities and boroughs in Ireland sending representatives to parliament, likewise copy of any letter or report received by the Chief Secretary, in answer to such instructions*, H.C. 1831–2, [519], xliii, p. 39.

22 O'Brien, *The Catholic middle classes*, p. 4.

23 Ian d'Alton, *Protestant society and politics in Cork, 1812–1844* (Cork, 1980) pp 93–100.

24 On the franchise, see Peter Jupp and Stephen Royle, 'The social geography of Cork City elections, 1801–30' in *Irish Historical Studies*, xxix, no. 113, (May 1994) pp 23–24.

25 O'Brien, *The Catholic middle classes*, p. 4.

26 O'Brien, *The Catholic middle classes*, pp 13–14.

27 *CMC* 28 August 1826.

28 Ian d'Alton, 'Keeping faith: An evocation of the Cork Protestant character, 1820–1920', in Cornelius Buttimer and Patrick O'Flanagan (eds.), *Cork: history and society* (Dublin, 1993) pp 765–767.

29 Sheahan, *Articles of Irish manufacture*, p. 94.

30 d'Alton, *Protestant society and politics in Cork*, p. 136.

31 Sheahan, *Articles of Irish manufacture*, p. 35; *CMC* 8 March 1830.

32 *CMC* 1 December 1826.

33 Sheahan, *Articles of Irish manufacture*, p. 35.

34 *List of freemen and freeholders, alphabetically arranged, who voted at the Cork election, December 1826*, p. 97.

35 *CMC* 14 November 1832.

36 *SR* April 1824.

37 O'Ferrall, *Catholic emancipation*, p. 66.

38 *CMC* 3 January 1827.

39 O'Ferrall, *Catholic emancipation*, p. 171.

40 *CMC* 21 August 1828.

41 *The Freeholder*, 29 December 1827.

42 *CMC* 5 November 1828.

43 *The Freeholder*, 29 December 1827; 9 January 1828.

44 *County of Clare election* (Cork, 1828) p. 83.

45 *County of Clare election*, p. 84.

46 Sheahan, *Articles of Irish manufacture*, pp 40–41. Daniel Casey, a well-known local wit and writer, was an uncle of Sir John Pope Hennessy (D.J. O'Donoghue, *The poets of Ireland* [Dublin, 1912] p. 62).

47 O'Ferrall, *Catholic emancipation*, p. 199.

48 *CMC* 17 October, 19 December 1828; *CC* 14 October 1828.

49 *County of Clare election*, p. 96.

50 *CC* 13 September 1828.

51 *CMC* 25 August 1828.

52 O'Ferrall, *Catholic emancipation*, p. 223.

53 *CMC* 21 August 1828.

54 *CMC* 25, 29 August 1828; Sheahan, *Articles of Irish manufacture*, p. 42.

55 *CMC* 29 August 1828.

56 *CMC* 26 November 1828.

57 Sheahan, *Articles of Irish manufacture*, p. 42; CAI, Day Papers, U140/26, Minutes of the committee meeting of 20 November 1828.

58 *CMC* 19, 26 November 1828.

59 *CMC* 5, 19, 26 November 1828; CAI, Day Papers, U140/18, Martin J. Farrell to J.J. Hayes, 28 September 1828.

60 O'Ferrall, *Catholic emancipation*, p. 225.

61 K.T. Hoppen, *Elections, politics and society in Ireland, 1832–1885* (Oxford, 1984) p. 1.

62 NLI, Wyse Papers, Ms. 15,023, Stephen Coppinger to Thomas Wyse, 23 March 1829.

63 Sheahan, *Articles of Irish manufacture*, p. 80.

64 Sheahan, *Articles of Irish manufacture*, p. 82.

65 Sheahan, *Articles of Irish manufacture*, p. 89.

66 d'Alton, *Protestant society and politics in Cork*, pp. 143–5.

67 Sheahan, *Articles of Irish manufacture*, pp 89–90.

68 Thomas Sheahan, 'Table-talk', *Irish Catholic Magazine*, July, August 1829.

69 Sheahan, *Articles of Irish manufacture*, p. 94.

70 Sheahan, *Articles of Irish manufacture*, pp 94–6.

71 Dan Meagher to Thomas Sheahan, 3 March 1830, published in C. B. Gibson, *The history of the county and city of Cork*, (2 vols, Cork, 1864) ii, p. 297.

THE TRADES, CHOLERA, AND THE
ELECTIONS IN 1832

1 John B. O'Brien, 'Population, politics and society in Cork, 1780–1900', in Buttimer and O'Flanagan (eds.), *Cork: history and society*, pp 703–704.

2 Raymond Crotty, *Irish agricultural production: its volume and structure* (Cork, 1966) p. 42.

3 Joel Mokyr and Cormac Ó Gráda, 'Poor and getting poorer? living standards in Ireland before the Famine', in *Economic History Review*, xli, no. 2, (1988) p. 211.

4 O'Brien, 'Population, politics and society in Cork', p. 704.

5 Conrad Gill, *The rise of the Irish linen industry* (Oxford, 1925) p. 324; Colin Rynne, *The industrial archaeology of Cork city and its environs* (Dublin, 1999) pp 96–8.

6 *First report of the royal commission into the condition of the poorer classes in Ireland. Appendix C – Part I*, p. 28.

7 Sheahan, *Irish destitution in 1834*, p. 19.

8 Andy Bielenberg, *Cork's industrial revolution, 1780–1880* (Cork, 1991) p. 23.

9 Cronin, *Country, class or craft?*, p. 21. By 1881 there were as few as seven weavers living in Cork city and none by the census of 1901.

10 Sheahan, *Irish destitution in 1834*, p. 22.

11 *First report of the royal commission into the condition of the poorer classes in Ireland. Appendix C – Part I*, p. 28.

12 The 1832 figures are more precise because Sheahan carried out a detailed survey of the city coopers in February that year.

13 *First report of the royal commission into the condition of the poorer classes in Ireland. Appendix C – Part I*, p. 27.

14 Cronin, *Country, class or craft?*, p. 32.

15 Sheahan, *Irish destitution in 1834*, pp 17–24.

16 Sheahan, *Irish destitution in 1834*, p. 24.

17 *CMC* 13 June 1832.

18 *CMC* 27 January, 1 February 1832.

19 *CMC* 1 February 1832.

20 R.J. Morris, *Cholera 1832: the social response to an epidemic* (London, 1976) pp 21–4; Richard Evans, *Death in Hamburg: society and politics in the cholera years, 1830–1910* (London, 1987) pp 226–7.

21 Evans, *Death in Hamburg*, pp 230–1.

22 *SR* 18 October 1831.

23 Evans, *Death in Hamburg*, p. 260.

24 Evans, *Death in Hamburg*, pp 243–4.

25 O'Mahony, *In the shadows*, p. 95.

26 *SR* 17 November 1831.

27 *SR* 10 November 1831.

28 *SR* 8, 12 November 1831.

29 *SR* 17, 19 November 1831.

30 *SR* 17 November 1831.

31 *CMC* 20 January 1832.

32 *CMC* 20 January 1832.

33 *CMC* 25, 27 January; 1 February 1832.

34 *CMC* 25 January 1832.

35 *CMC* 10, 15 February 1832.

36 *CMC* 10 February 1832.

37 *CMC* 20 January 1832.

38 NA, CSORP (1832) 1412.

39 *CMC* 10 February 1832.

40 *CMC* 25 January 1832.

41 *CMC* 27 January 1832.

42 *CMC* 27 January 1832.

43 Sheahan, *Irish destitution in 1834*, pp 25–27.

44 *CMC* 1 February 1832.

45 Sheahan, *Articles of Irish manufacture*, pp 183–90.

46 *SR* 13, 18 October 1831.

47 *CMC* 19 March 1832.

48 *CMC* 19, 21 March 1832.

49 *CMC* 19, 21 March 1832.

50 *CMC* 4 June 1832.

51 *CMC* 25 April 1832.

52 *CMC* 27 April 1832.

53 *CMC* 27 April 1832.

54 *First report of the royal commission into the condition of the poorer classes in Ireland. Appendix C – Part I*, p. 24. For a useful survey of the progress of the 1832–33 cholera epidemic in Cork see, O'Mahony, *In the shadows*, pp. 94–107.

55 Evans, *Death in Hamburg*, p. 260.

56 *CMC* 27 April, 7 May 1832.

57 *First report of the royal commission into the condition of the poorer classes in Ireland. Appendix C – Part I*, p. 24.

58 *CMC* 2 May 1832.

59 *CMC* 7 May 1832.

60 *CMC* 13 June 1832.

61 *Weekly Dublin Satirist* 4 April 1835; *CMC* 13, 18 June 1832. By 1832, however, Daly was resident in Bridge Street.

62 *CMC* 8, 13 June 1832; *Pigot's directory of 1824*, pp. 249–250, 254.

63 *CMC* 13 June 1832.

64 *CMC* 25, 27 June; 16 July; 1, 8, 15, 17, 24 August; 5 September 1832.

65 *The appeal of the national association for the encouragement, promotion and consumption of Irish produce and manufacture* (Dublin, 1832); *CMC* 7, 12 September 1832.

66 Sheahan, *Irish destitution in 1834*, p. 13.

67 *CMC* 19 November 1832.

68 CC 14 June 1832.

69 *CMC* 25 June 1832. Warren's Place is now known as Parnell Place.

70 *CMC* 25 June 1832.

71 *CMC* 25, 27 June 1832. Also, see unpaginated advertisements at the back of Sheahan, *Articles of Irish manufacture*.

72 *CMC* 11 June 1832.

73 *CMC* 27 June 1832.

74 *CMC* 27 June 1832.

75 *CMC* 27 June 1832.

76 *CMC* 3 October 1832; *First report of the royal commission into the condition of the poorer classes in Ireland. Appendix C – Part I*, p. 28.

77 *CMC* 16 July; 1, 8 August, 1832.

78 *CMC* 15 August; 7, 19 September 1832.

79 *CMC* 13 August 1832.

80 *SR* 1 February 1831.

81 *CMC* 15 August 1832.

82 *SR* 13 November 1830.

83 *CMC* 22, 24 August 1832.

84 *CMC* 14 November 1832.

85 *Weekly Dublin Satirist*, 28 March 1835.

86 *CMC* 17 October 1832.

87 *CMC* 17 August 1832.

88 *CMC* 17 October 1832.

89 *CMC* 19 October 1832.

90 *CMC* 24 October 1832.

91 *CMC* 26 October 1832.

92 *CMC* 17 October 1832.

93 *CMC* 2 November 1832.

94 d'Alton, *Protestant society and politics in Cork*, p. 150.

95 Gibson, *History of the county and city of Cork*, ii, p. 300.

96 d'Alton, *Protestant society and politics in Cork*, pp 159–160.

97 *CMC* 7 November 1832.

98 *CMC* 14 November 1832.

99 *CMC* 14 November 1832.

100 *CMC* 21, 23, 28 November 1832.

101 *CMC* 23 January 1833.

102 *CMC* 7 December 1832.

103 *CMC* 5 December 1832.

104 *CMC* 10, 12 December 1832.

105 *CMC* 12 December 1832.

106 *CMC* 21 December 1832.

107 *CMC* 21 December 1832.

REPEAL AND THE CORK
WORKING CLASS

1 Eric Glasgow and Donald Read, *Feargus O'Connor: Irishman and Chartist* (London, 1961) pp 28–31; W. J. O'Neill Daunt, *Ireland and her agitators* (Dublin, 1867) pp 104–9; *CMC* 20 August 1832.

2 *CMC* 26 December 1832.

3 *CMC* 31 December 1832.

4 *CMC* 31 December 1832.

5 *CMC* 2 January 1833.

6 *CMC* 2 January 1833.

7 *CMC* 4, 16, 18 January 1833.

8 *CMC* 16 January 1833.

9 d'Alton, 'Keeping faith: An evocation of the Cork Protestant character, 1820–1920', pp 767–9.

10 *CMC* 20 February 1833.

11 *CMC* 22 February 1833.

12 *CMC* 25, 27 March 1833.
13 *CC* 26 March 1833; *CMC* 29 January 1834.
14 Bielenberg, *Cork's industrial revolution*, p. 64; *CMC* 20 January 1832.
15 *CMC* 20 January 1832.
16 Thomas Sheahan, 'Memoir of William Ring', *CMC* 29 January 1834.
17 *CMC* 25 March 1833.
18 Ó Tuathaigh, *Ireland before the famine*, p. 169.
19 Virginia Crossman, *Politics, law and order in nineteenth-century Ireland* (Dublin, 1996) pp 62–3.
20 *CMC* 17 April 1833.
21 Oliver MacDonagh, *The emancipist: Daniel O'Connell, 1830–1847* (London, 1989) pp 92–3.
22 *CMC* 12 April 1833.
23 MacDonagh, *The emancipist*, p. 95.
24 *CMC* 13 June 1833.
25 *CMC* 14 June 1833.
26 *CMC* 14 June 1833.
27 MacDonagh, *The emancipist*, pp 95–7.
28 Fergus D'Arcy, 'The artisans of Dublin and Daniel O'Connell, 1830–47: an unquiet liaison,' in *Irish Historical Studies*, xvii, no. 66 (September 1970) pp 226–227.
29 MacDonagh, *The emancipist*, p. 98.
30 *CMC* 15 November 1833.
31 Sheahan, *Irish destitution in 1834*, pp 14–15; *CMC* 15 November 1833.
32 Emmet O'Connor, *A labour history of Ireland, 1824–1960* (Dublin, 1992) pp 6–14.
33 Sheahan, *Irish destitution in 1834*, p. 14.
34 Sheahan, *Irish destitution in 1834*, p. 14.
35 A useful survey of trades organisation in Cork city is Seán Daly, 'The trades of Cork, 1700–1870' which is published as an appendix to Sean Daly, *Cork, a city in crisis: a history of labour conflict and social misery, 1870–1872* (Cork, 1978) pp 253–314.
36 *CMC* 15 November 1833.
37 *CC* 17 January 1833.
38 *CMC* 18, 20 March 1833.
39 *CMC* 19 June 1833.
40 *CMC* 15 November 1833.
41 *CMC* 15 November 1833.
42 *CMC* 6, 13, 30 December 1833; 6 January, 11 April, 11 June 1834.
43 *PP* 6 December 1834; *CMC* 13 January, 26 March, 4 April, 1, 8 August, 3 December 1834; 1 April, 25 September 1835; *CEH* 21, 23, 30 March 1836.
44 Daly, 'The trades of Cork, 1700–1870', pp 282–3.
45 *CMC* 13 February 1835.
46 *CMC* 3 January, 12, 19, 21 February, 2, 9 April, 11 July, 3 December 1834.
47 *First report of the royal commission into the condition of the poorer classes in Ireland. Appendix C – Part I*, pp 23, 28; Sheahan, *Irish destitution in 1834*, passim.
48 Sheahan, *Irish destitution in 1834*, pp 18–19, 21–2.
49 *CMC* 8 October 1834.
50 *CMC* 13, 15, 17 October 1834.
51 *CMC* 26 January; *PP* 31 January, 11 April 1835.
52 *CMC* 19 January 1835.
53 *CMC* 10 September 1834; 15 April 1835.
54 *PP* 15 August, 5, 19 December 1835.
55 *PP* 4, 18 July 1835; *CMC* 13, 19, 26 February, 4, 11 March 1835.
56 *CMC* 13 February 1835.
57 *CMC* 26 February, 4 March 1835.
58 *CMC* 29 July, 3 August 1835.
59 Crossman, *Politics, law and order in nineteenth century Ireland*, p. 69.
60 *SR* 31 March 1836.
61 *SR* 31 March 1836.
62 *SR* 5 April 1836.
63 *SR* 5 April 1836.
64 *SR* 16 April 1836.

CONCLUSION

1 *SR* 31 March 1836.
2 *CMC* 4 March 1835.
3 On the Peoples Hall see Maura Murphy, 'Repeal and Young Ireland in Cork politics, 1830–50', (MA thesis, UCC, 1975); and Maura Cronin, *Country, class or craft?*, p. 102.
4 Maura Murphy, 'Municipal reform and the repeal movement in Cork, 1833–1844', in *Journal of the Cork historical and archaeological society*, lxxxi, no. 233 (1976) p. 10.

Maynooth Research Guides for Irish Local History

IN THIS SERIES

1   Raymond Refaussé, *Church of Ireland Records*
2   Terry Dooley, *Sources for the History of Landed estates in Ireland*
3   Patrick J. Corish and David Sheehy, *Records of the Irish Catholic Church*
4   Jacinta Prunty, *Maps and Mapmaking in Local History*

Maynooth Studies in Irish Local History

IN THIS SERIES

1   Paul Connell, *Parson, Priest and Master: National Education in Co. Meath 1824–41*

2   Denis A. Cronin, *A Galway Gentleman in the Age of Improvement: Robert French of Monivea, 1716–79*

3   Brian Ó Dálaigh, *Ennis in the 18th Century: Portrait of an Urban Community*

4   Séamas Ó Maitiú, *The Humours of Donnybrook: Dublin's Famous Fair and its Suppression*

5   David Broderick, *An Early Toll-Road: The Dublin–Dunleer Turnpike, 1731–1855*

6   John Crawford, *St Catherine's Parish, Dublin 1840–1900: Portrait of a Church of Ireland Community*

7   William Gacquin, *Roscommon Before the Famine: The Parishes of Kiltoom and Cam, 1749–1845*

8   Francis Kelly, *Window on a Catholic Parish: St Mary's Granard, Co. Longford, 1933–68*

9   Charles V. Smith, *Dalkey: Society and Economy in a Small Medieval Irish Town*

10   Desmond J. O'Dowd, *Changing Times: Religion and Society in Nineteenth-Century Celbridge*

11   Proinnsíos Ó Duigneáin, *The Priest and the Protestant Woman*

12   Thomas King, *Carlow: the manor and town, 1674–1721*

13   Joseph Byrne, *War and Peace: The Survival of the Talbots of Malahide 1641–1671*

14   Bob Cullen, *Thomas L. Synnott: The Career of a Dublin Catholic 1830–70*

15   Helen Sheil, *Falling into Wretchedness: Ferbane in the late 1830s*

16   Jim Gilligan, *Graziers and Grasslands: Portrait of a Rural Meath Community 1854–1914*

17   Miriam Lambe, *A Tipperary Estate: Castle Otway, Templederry 1750–1853*

18   Liam Clare, *Victorian Bray: A Town Adapts to Changing Times*

Maynooth Studies in Irish Local History (cont.)